TAKING DOMESTIC VIOLENCE
SERIOUSLY:

Issues for the
Civil and Criminal Justice System

MONICA McWILLIAMS
and
LYNDA SPENCE

TAKING DOMESTIC VIOLENCE SERIOUSLY:

Issues for the
Civil and Criminal Justice System

A report to the Northern Ireland Office

MONICA McWILLIAMS and LYNDA SPENCE

Centre for Research on Women
University of Ulster
Jordanstown
BT37 0QB

February 1996

Belfast: The Stationery Office

Published and Printed in the United Kingdom by The Stationery Office Limited

Contents

Acknowledgements

We would like to thank all those groups and individuals, throughout Northern Ireland who participated in this study. The Director of Public Prosecutions lent his support to this project and for this we are most appreciative. We are particularly grateful to John Rea and the staff in the Department of Public Prosecutions, without whose assistance we would have been unable to access the material used in this study.

Other relevant material was provided by Michael Patterson, Senior Assistant Statistician, RUC and his colleague Pamela Morton. We thank them for their cooperative and efficient responses to numerous requests for material on Northern Ireland's crime statistics. We are also grateful to the statisticians in police forces elsewhere for the comparative material which they helped to provide: Catherine Archer and John Scothern of West Yorkshire Police Statistics Branch; Christopher Sheridan of the Garda Siochana Crime Branch; Pat Climo and Michael Stevens of Devon and Cornwall Police Statistics Branch.

We acknowledge the assistance provided by the Northern Ireland Court Service and in particular, William Hanna, Deputy Director of NICS. Thanks are due also to the Clerks of Court, their staff at the various Magistrates Courts and the magistrates and court officials who gave up time to be interviewed. Particular thanks are due to RUC Chief Superintendent, Tom King and his colleagues, Peter Kane and Eddie Mercer, who have a particular expertise in this field. Margo Hesketh and Cecilia Whitehorn from Women's Aid contributed many important insights from their work on domestic violence.

Thanks are due also to Lorraine Majury and Morag Stark for their administrative and secretarial assistance. Celia Davies, former Director of the Centre for Research on Women at the University of Ulster and Clare Archbold, Lecturer in Law at Queen's University provided helpful and valuable comments on the report.

In the on-going work for this study, we came in contact with a number of individuals who had a particular interest in the project. Some spoke of their personal experiences and demonstrated

incredible resilience in the face of ongoing and persistent abuse. To them we owe a particular thanks.

We are grateful to the Northern Ireland Office for funding this study, especially Tom Haire for supporting the proposal from its initial stage. The opinions and recommendations expressed in this book are the responsibility of the researchers and not the Northern Ireland Office.

MONICA McWILLIAMS

Senior Lecturer

University of Ulster

LYNDA SPENCE

Research Officer

Centre for Research on Women

University of Ulster

Executive Summary

This report sets out the findings of the civil law and criminal justice system's response to domestic violence in Northern Ireland. It involves the police, lawyers, court officials, members of the judiciary and those working within the court and probation services. It is of particular relevance to all who are tasked with the responsibility of providing protection and safety for victims. It addresses questions about what should happen to those who persist in perpetrating domestic violence and outlines responses to offenders from both within Northern Ireland and elsewhere.

An extensive literature in the United Kingdom, the USA and elsewhere is reviewed. The review pays particular attention to the way in which domestic violence is responded to by the police and how these incidents are subsequently processed. Particular problems in relation to prosecution and sentencing are highlighted. We note the extent and nature of domestic violence, as it presents to the police and courts, but emphasise that this is an exploratory project rather than a representative study. Having said that the material does provide a useful insight into the various ways in which domestic violence is dealt with by the civil and criminal justice system; it highlights the problems in the current system and points to the need to take this issue seriously. We outline below a list of points which demonstrate this.

Statistics Recorded by Police and Courts

- Between 1990-1994, 21 women were killed by their partners in Northern Ireland. This represents 48 per cent of all women murdered during this five year period. In contrast, 8 per cent of all male homicides (seven out of 83) were domestic violence related.

- In 1991 there were six women killed by their partners in Northern Ireland. In the same year, there were 120 female domestic violence homicides in England and Wales. Proportionate to the size of the population, the Northern Ireland figure is relatively high.

- At least 23 per cent of all homicides in Northern Ireland occur in the context of an intimate personal relationship between two adults. If others killed at the same time as the partner, in the domestic violence incident, are added to this figure it would mean that more than one in four homicides are due to domestic violence in Northern Ireland.

- There were 29 domestic violence killings in Northern Ireland compared to ten in the Republic of Ireland in the five year period 1990-1994.

- The spousal homicide rate for Northern Ireland is 1.9. This is the number of partners killed per hundred thousand married or cohabiting couples in the country. The Northern Ireland figure is higher than that reported for countries such as Canada and the Republic of Ireland.

- More women than men are killed. The Northern Ireland sex ratio of domestic violence homicides is 3:1. Where women kill, there is generally a previous history of domestic violence by the man on his female partner.

- An important feature to note in domestic violence cases in which women have been killed is that a significant proportion of the deceased have left the relationship or are in the process of separation. Data recording mechanisms need to record residency status in homicide cases so that the extent to which this phenomenon occurs in the United Kingdom can be better analysed.

Taking Figures for One Year

- In 1994, there were 360 serious assaults on women by their partners, and five attempted murders. These figures relate only to reported assaults and hence under-estimate the extent of these attacks.

- According to official police statistics, on average, one woman is seriously assaulted (with AOABH, GBH or attempted murder) by her male partner every day in Northern Ireland.

Policing of Domestic Violence Incidents in Northern Ireland

- The arrest rate for reported domestic violence incidents is between 12 per cent and 16 per cent in Northern Ireland.

- Only 11 per cent of police cases in domestic violence proceed to prosecution.

- Police officers attend just under 3,000 incidents of domestic violence in Northern Ireland annually.

Prosecution

- Two-thirds of all male-female violence recorded by the courts is domestic violence.

- Fourteen percent of all Offences Against the Person cases in five magistrates courts were domestic violence related. If figures could be obtained for criminal damage and Breach of the Peace cases which occur in the context of domestic violence together with breaches of personal protection and exclusion orders, then the extent of domestic violence in Magistrate's Courts could be more accurately assessed.

- Approximately one-third of all cases are withdrawn from prosecution at the Magistrates Court. Various reasons are put forward to explain this high withdrawal rate but this clearly is a subject for further investigation.

- At the Crown Court in six of the ten cases in which the police charged men with murder, the charge was either reduced or the offender was found guilty of the lesser charge of manslaughter. Issues about what constitutes diminished responsibility and provocation in the context of domestic violence are highlighted here.

- The decision to review charges, which can lead to a reduced charge and a lighter sentence, also arises in the prosecution of domestic violence cases in which men were initially charged with attempted murder. Only one out of the nine cases returned a verdict of attempted murder in the court proceedings recorded here. The issue of proving intent in domestic violence cases is discussed.

Sentencing

- Offenders rarely receive custodial sentences in domestic violence cases heard in Magistrates Courts. The more serious assault cases appear to be prosecuted through the use of suspended sentences and fines.

- Prosecution outcomes such as a fine or 'bind over' suggest that cases involving domestic violence are being treated differently than prosecutions for similar types of assault which involve strangers.

Issues Raised by Research

- Offences which increase in frequency and intensity need to be taken more seriously by those responding to domestic violence. The previous history of the offender's abusive behaviour towards his partner is an important factor and, as such, it needs to be an important part of the discussions pertaining to prosecution and sentencing. Evidence presented here points to cases in which men who have killed their partners have previously been prosecuted for less serious offences. Where fatalities occur, the onus is clearly on the criminal justice system to work towards the development of a more preventative policy on domestic violence.

- Clearly there is good practice, and examples of this are documented. Suggestions are put forward on a more coordinated approach to victims who report domestic violence but remain concerned about following through with prosecution.

- There are 12 recommendations in all. These highlight the need for an overall policy framework, for training, for improved guidelines for police and prosecutors and for specific crime statistics. Above all, a more integrated criminal justice response to domestic violence is recommended.

ONE

Introduction

Domestic violence is not something new. As long ago as the fourteenth century, reference was made to a case of a woman seeking refuge from her abusive husband. However, at that time and until relatively recently, domestic violence was untouched by law and protected as part of the private sphere of family life. Over the last twenty years as it has become more visible and has been recognised as a feature of contemporary family life, domestic violence is no longer perceived as a purely 'private' problem. There has been an explosion of legal reform and social service efforts; the development of refuges and helplines; the production of government reports and research studies; extensive coverage of trials and front page headlines in media reports; and public awareness campaigns which have led to a recognition of domestic violence as a 'public harm'. Moreover, a recent report in Great Britain concluded that domestic violence was amongst the most serious of our national social problems, important not only for the suffering it caused but for its effect on the community as a whole (Victim Support 1992).

At the same time, there has also been social resistance to change. Although domestic violence has evolved from a 'private' to a more 'public' issue, it has remained a divisive issue amongst policy-makers and help-providers. Abuse which occurs in the context of people's own homes is deeply threatening. It challenges our most fundamental assumptions about the nature of intimate relations and the safety of family life. By seeing such abuse as 'private' we affirm it as a problem that is individual, that only involves a particular male-female relationship, and for which there is no social responsibility to remedy. However, a concept of privacy which says that what goes on in a violent relationship should not be the subject of state or community intervention has begun to change.

Background to the study

As a result of concerted mobilisation by both voluntary and statutory agencies in Northern Ireland, important legislative changes

have taken place. These include the introduction of injunctions against violent partners, excluding them from the family home and making breaches of injunctions an arrestable offence. Important policy measures have also been developed relating to procedures for the police in investigating incidences of violence in the home. It is against this background that the present research was commissioned by the Northern Ireland Office.

The research responds to the need to provide an analysis of the nature and extent of domestic violence within both civil law and the criminal justice system in Northern Ireland. The proposal that projects like this should be undertaken was first put forward in a research study on domestic violence commissioned by the DHSS in 1992.[1] Since then, a government policy statement 'Tackling Domestic Violence' has identified, amongst other things, the need to improve the information base and to raise awareness amongst the public and professionals of the extent and seriousness of domestic violence. An interdepartmental group, which was formed as a result of the DHSS research to develop policy and principles for those working in the field of domestic violence, recommended that a Domestic Violence Regional Forum be established to take these issues forward. This has now been set up.

Objectives of this study

The main focus of this study is to provide research-based analyses and information on the impact and effectiveness of legal and criminal justice agencies' responses to domestic violence. The objectives are:

1. to provide a critical commentary on existing research literature on domestic violence, relating to police practice and the component elements of the criminal justice process;

2. to examine the extent and range of domestic violence records retained by the Department of Public Prosecutions, police, courts and other available resources;

3. to explore the incidence, levels and trends of crime related to domestic violence;

---

1   This research was published the following year: McWilliams, M. and McKiernan, J. (1993) *Bringing It Out In The Open: Domestic Violence in Northern Ireland*, Belfast: HMSO.

4. to appraise the support for any recommendations that arise from the research, particularly in relation to civil remedies, cautioning, arrest procedures and sentencing.

Definitions of Domestic Violence

For the purposes of this study, domestic violence is defined as the intentional physical, mental or sexual abuse or the threat of injury or harm by a current or former partner. The issue of what constitutes mental harm in this context remains problematic particularly since legal instruments have been drawn up in different ways. What most researchers are agreed on is that domestic violence is most frequently perpetrated by men; that it is intentional and that it involves force and coercion. The extent to which women use violence against their partners, however, is also discussed in this study. Also included are couples who are not legally married as well as those who have been living apart. The determining feature is that there has, at some time, been an intimate sexual relationship with the person who has carried out the abuse.

The definition, as used here, does not include acts of violence which take place between other family members. For various reasons the use of the term 'domestic' can sometimes be misleading. However, it is the term most frequently used in policy-making and is chosen here in preference to terms such as family violence, spouse abuse, wife abuse or battered women.

Rationale for this study

One of the basic questions which concerns those dealing with domestic violence is: "why does it occur?" Why do so many serious assaults take place between people who are bound to each through love and marriage? Given that we are reporting on the criminal justice response, it is particularly important to offer some rationale as to why such behaviour becomes unacceptable and constitutes a criminal offence. We can only briefly touch on this here since this report is targeted at the response to domestic violence and not necessarily to its causes. However, what one believes to be the cause of a problem can determine how one tries to resolve the problem. Consequently, we briefly outline some of the reasons put forward to explain why domestic violence occurs.

Dobash and Dobash (1992) argue that there are four main sources of conflict which lead to violent attacks by men on women with whom they are in intimate relationships. These are:

- possessiveness and jealousy;

- men's expectations concerning women's domestic work;

- men's sense of right to punish 'their' women for perceived wrong-doing;

- the importance to men of maintaining or exercising their positions of authority.

Mooney (1994) in a recent study of domestic violence in Islington, London, presented 500 men with a number of stereotypical situations based on the sources of conflict outlined above. She found that 19 per cent of men stated that they had acted violently at least once within the range of incidents presented to them and concluded that where women fail to perform what are perceived as their duties in the area of domestic and sexual services, they can be severely at risk of physical abuse.

Given the context of this study, and the fact that we have not undertaken any fieldwork with the victims, we do not attempt to confirm the extent to which the above factors occurred in the various incidents referred to in this report. Instead, we show the variable responses that are currently taking place within the civil, legal and criminal justice system and put forward arguments which point to the need to take domestic violence much more seriously than at present. We show, for instance, how women who have left relationships require greater protection and safety, particularly since the threat of leaving the relationship can in itself cause an escalation in the level of life threatening assaults. What we attempt to do throughout the report is to highlight the problems which victims, police officers and prosecutors face in responding effectively to domestic violence. At the same time, we hope to show that it is possible to find alternatives to what on occasions may seem difficult and dangerous issues. The report highlights the strengths and weaknesses of the current legal system and points to examples of what might constitute elements of good practice amongst the various practitioners.

In collecting the information for this report, we talked to magistrates, clerks of court, prosecutors, lawyers, police officers at both

policy and operational level, Women's Aid workers and police statisticians. With the assistance of the Department of Public Prosecutions and the Northern Ireland Court Service, data were collected on crimes related to domestic violence at both the Magistrates and Crown courts. We made some attempt to include the victims' perspective by observing the domestic proceedings court and by speaking directly to a limited number of women who had pursued their cases through the criminal court. This side of the picture needs to be augmented by a further study. The extent to which victims feel enabled to seek help from the current system, both in terms of policing and prosecution, and the extent to which they feel confident after having sought justice might be one follow-up to this particular study. The material documented here points to the reasons why such a study should be carried out.

Structure of the report

The main elements of this research are an extensive literature review and analyses of records held by the civil and criminal justice agencies. In the following chapter we present the findings from a range of studies on police and justice responses to domestic violence in the United States, Canada and Great Britain. This literature makes it clear that both the judicial system and the police, operating with the authority of the state, have a major role to play not just in providing assistance to victims of domestic violence but in driving forward policy in this area. As Dobash and Dobash (1992) note

'Attempting to employ the law and the justice system to assist abused women is a historically rooted strategy which implicitly or explicitly accepts the enabling aspects of the state as the means of redressing the violent injustices and imbalances of power within the family...state intervention remains one of the primary vehicles for attempting to redress injustices in advanced industrial societies.'

Our attempt to see how the law and justice system respond to domestic violence in the specific context of Northern Ireland is presented in the subsequent chapters of the report. First, we provide data from 1990 to 1994 on the number of homicides, recorded under the Offences Against the Person Act, which have been the result of domestic violence. Figures are also provided for a few other areas so that an attempt can be made at gauging the extent of fatalities in Northern Ireland compared to elsewhere. Chapter 3 also shows the

outcomes of the prosecutions for murder, manslaughter and attempted murder cases as well as the serious charges for assaults relating to domestic violence over a three year period.

Chapter 4 then reports on observations, interviews, and analysis of records in five Magistrates courts. This chapter deals with the incidence of domestic violence cases in these courts and of the range of sentencing for this type of offence. Chapter 5 concentrates on personal protection and exclusion orders which are dealt with under civil legislation. It provides data on the prosecutions related to the breaches of these orders at Magistrates courts. The RUC's policy on domestic violence and the way in which police officers have been responding to incidents of domestic violence are dealt with in Chapter 6. Finally, the conclusions and recommendations are presented.

TWO

Domestic Violence and the Criminal Justice System: A Literature Review

Research on domestic violence has grown at a very rapid rate in the last decade, faster, some have argued, than in any other substantive area of the social sciences (Gelles and Conte 1990). Here, we review the research evidence from a range of countries in an attempt to assess the effectiveness of criminal justice intervention in relation to domestic violence. First, we examine the various police responses to domestic violence in North America and Great Britain. Then we turn to the prosecution system to examine the criminal law in each of these jurisdictions and to draw on examples of good practice where these exist. Finally, we review the literature on the impact of civil law in relation to domestic violence. A separate chapter of the report is devoted to policing in Northern Ireland (see Chapter 6), and where we discuss the civil legislation, we comment only on the literature from Great Britain and Northern Ireland.

Policing

Reporting domestic violence

The first point to note is that domestic violence is a greatly under-reported crime. Even when it is reported there is a lack of accuracy in the way in which it is recorded. In the United States, Buzawa and Buzawa (1992) state that estimates vary widely but appear to confirm that in the past, somewhat less than 10 per cent of domestic violence incidents were ever reported to the police. A Canadian study (Jaffe et al. 1986) estimated that women were assaulted on average 35 times before contacting the police. However, there is evidence from the British Crime Surveys that attitudes towards the reporting of domestic violence are changing: in 1981 about one-fifth of women who suffered domestic assaults said that they had reported at least one incident to the police whereas in 1987 half of them said they had (Davidoff and Dowds 1989). Nonetheless, these researchers note a large discrepancy between the British Crime

Survey estimates of the number of domestic assaults and the much smaller number of police recorded 'notifiable' domestic assaults. The way in which the police record incidents of domestic violence has been a focus of much criticism by both researchers and practitioners and is a point to which we will return later. It is worth noting at this point however, that the Metropolitan Police Commissioner claimed that some of the 6.9 per cent increase in violent crime in the 1994 Home Office Notifiable Offences figures was attributable to 'a harder line' being taken by police on domestic violence attackers (*Guardian*, 12.4.95).

The Police Response

The police may be viewed by victims of domestic violence as the most accessible agency, available on a 24 hour basis. As such, they perform the role of gatekeeper, not only to the criminal justice system but to other helping agencies. Much of the literature in both Britain and America has focused on the police response, of which it has frequently been highly critical.

United States

Available research suggests that historically, the police response to calls in cases of wife abuse has been less than adequate, largely because of a preferred policy of non-intervention. Buzawa and Buzawa (1993) attribute the police reluctance to be involved to:

(1) *Organisational Issues*, such as limitations on police powers of arrest; the demands of domestic violence cases on police time; inadequate information systems which did not alert officers to prior offender histories; and poor training.

(2) *Police Attitudes* towards intervention, which included cynicism, social class stereotyping of victims and assailants, fears for their own safety, as well as a preference for 'handling the situation' by 'taking charge', rather than defining their role in terms of enforcing the law; and a belief that such cases are not 'real' police work.

Ferraro (1989) also notes that even when there is a stated police policy of intervention on domestic violence, such as an overt pro-arrest policy, police on the ground find ways of circumventing such policies.

Police intervention in domestic violence has notably changed over the last two decades. In the 1970s, the New York City Police Department, like most American police forces at that time, emphasised mediation and conflict resolution tactics in training officers on domestic violence. This approach has since been overturned by a movement towards a punishment orientation for domestic violence. Commentators trace this to a combination of grass roots and feminist activism calling for more rigorous treatment of perpetrators and to the results of research on pro-arrest policies (Dobash and Dobash 1992; Buzawa and Buzawa 1993).

The most influential research, a catalyst for rapid change, was the Minneapolis Domestic Violence Experiment study (Sherman and Berk 1984). It was the first controlled, randomised test of the effectiveness of arrest for any offence. Misdemeanour domestic assault offenders in two precincts were randomly assigned to one of three experimental conditions: arrest, separation from the victim or advice/mediation. There was a six-month follow-up period when interviews were conducted with victims and offenders and official records of subsequent incidents were studied. The analysis of these data showed that those who were arrested had the lowest rate of recidivism (10 per cent) and those who were separated had the highest (24 per cent).

In 1984, the United States Attorney General's Task Force on Family Violence report had called for criminal justice agencies to respond to domestic violence as a criminal activity. By January 1987, 176 cities across the United States were using some form of arrest policy for domestic violence. Other factors prompting change were cases brought against police departments by battered wives for failure to protect them. A pivotal case was that of Thurman v. City of Torrington 1985, where Tracy Thurman accepted an out of court settlement of $1.9 million after being permanently injured by her estranged husband, following numerous fruitless calls for assistance to the police department. Gelles (1993) attributes the change in policy also to 'the advocacy of a control model of intervention ... during the period of political conservatism' (during the Reagan years) and 'repeated calls for strict and severe controls to punish all violent crime, not just family violence'.

Gelles also states that while the empirical results of the Minneapolis study were impressive, there was little theoretical justification to

explain why mandatory arrest would actually deter violent men. Arguing that the deterrence claim 'may well be the social science equivalent of cold fusion' (a much heralded research project which promised much but delivered nothing), he criticizes the internal and external validity of the study and reviews three replication studies funded by the United States National Institute of Justice. Dunford, Huizinga and Elliott's study (1990) in Omaha, Nebraska found that contrary to the evidence from Minneapolis, arrest together with an immediate period of custody was not a deterrent to continued domestic violence. Two interesting findings of this study were first, that arrest did not appear to place victims in greater danger of increased violence than the other alternatives and, secondly, that suspects who had left the scene of the crime but for whom arrest warrants were nonetheless issued had lower prevalence and frequency of repeat offending. The Charlotte, North Carolina, study (Hirschell et al. 1990) concluded that arrest was not a more effective deterrent to repeat abuse than other police responses. The Milwaukee study by Sherman et al. (1990) found that arrest delayed the average time until the next incident of violence, but did not directly affect the likelihood of future violence. However, offenders who were employed were less likely to re-offend than those who were unemployed, a finding reiterated by the Dade County Study (Pate and Hamilton 1992).

Schmidt and Sherman (1993) state that researchers in Colorado Springs and Metro-Dade found some support for the Minneapolis findings but only with limited measures. Their overall conclusion from a range of studies was that arrest

- has a different effect on offenders from different households;

- reduces domestic violence in some cities but increases it in others;

- reduces it amongst the employed but increases it in the unemployed;

- reduces it in the short term but can increase it in the long run.

They also argued that police can predict which couples are most likely to suffer future violence but that society values privacy too highly to encourage preventive action focusing on these couples. These writers call for a repeal of mandatory arrest laws, a return to police discretion and a focus on chronically violent couples.

Clearly, the inconsistent results of the Minneapolis domestic violence experiment and its replications have posed problems for researchers and policy-makers. There is however still support in the literature for pro-arrest policies. Berk (1993) argues that 'one can on the average do no better' than arrest. Stark (1993) while sharing reservations about the methodological flaws in both the original and replication studies, challenges negative views of mandatory arrest and the related argument that the criminal justice system should no longer be the focal point of society's response to domestic violence. He identifies violence against women as a civil rights issue, since the use of control and violence exploits sexual inequality and obstructs women's self-determination. Mandatory arrest controls police behaviour, sets a public standard for policy response, offers immediate protection from current violence and 'represents a progressive redistribution of justice on behalf of women'. Stark also points out that the replication studies results could be interpreted to indicate that arrest, without serious follow up and in isolation from other sanctions, is ineffective.

Polsby (1992) criticizes the narrow analysis of the replication studies and their failure to consider the dynamics of domestic violence as a process rather than a single incident. The studies had suggested a potential short-term deterrent effect on previously undeterred offenders, and the temporary cessation of violence 'should be viewed as a window of opportunity for other interventions'. Similarly, Bowman (1992) argues that the studies' quantitative methodology of isolating arrest as a factor in their experimental design distorts reality by failing to investigate other factors (such as prosecution) which may have a bearing on recidivism. She points out that these studies also omitted the opinions and perspectives of the women victims and asks: 'What might they say if they were offered both arrest and a variety of supportive services?' Bowman's argument is that arrest delivers an empowering message to the victim and communicates society's condemnation of abusive behaviour; this is supported by Lerman (1992) but she calls for more experiments which take account of the context in which arrests take place and which include variables such as:

- the victims' wishes and conduct;

- the behaviour of the police at the scene;

- whether or how cases are prosecuted and

- the sanctions, if any, which are imposed.

In relation to sanctions, the Charlotte study found that 65 per cent of the cases did not result in prosecution and less than one per cent of the convicted offenders received jail sentences (Hirschell *et al.* 1990). However there was no information about the deterrent effect or otherwise of those prosecutions that did occur. Calling for a co-ordinated response to domestic violence by the criminal justice system and social services, Lerman (1992) concludes that the replication studies should 'lead us to worry about communities in which the police are required to make arrests but in which the state takes no post-arrest action to protect the victim from further assaults'. This particular issue will be taken up later in our discussion on prosecution and sentencing but for now we will continue to examine police action on domestic violence by turning to the situation in Great Britain.

Great Britain

Following the report of the 1975 Parliamentary Select Committee on Violence in Marriage and its recommendations concerning housing and safety, legislation was passed in England and Wales, chiefly the 1976 Domestic Violence and Matrimonial Proceedings Act and the 1978 Domestic Proceedings and Magistrates Courts Act. Similar legislation was later enacted in Scotland and Northern Ireland. These Acts were designed to provide wives (and later co-habitees) with protection, including injunctions and exclusion orders against violent partners and the right to occupy the matrimonial home. The existing Offences against the Person Act (1861) continued to be the means of prosecuting criminal offences of common assault and the more serious violent attacks. Although the new legislation sought to address the problems of domestic violence, there were no recommendations at that stage for changes in police practice. Researchers in the United Kingdom subsequently raised concerns about police behaviour similar to those voiced by American researchers.

Parker (1985) noted the large gap between the law on the books and the law in action. Maidment (1985) felt that the promises of legal protection for battered women offered by the legislative reforms of the 1970s had not been fulfilled in practice and Faragher (1985), depicting the police as 'the point of access and a signpost to other sources of assistance', felt that their actions may be of crucial importance in signalling society's support for the victim or the lack

of it. Faragher's observational study of 26 domestic violence cases in Staffordshire indicated that arrest was used only infrequently (in two cases) by the police, although there was a clear infringement of the law in ten cases. Binney *et al.* (1981) found an arrest rate of only 20 per cent, even after life-threatening assaults. In her study conducted in two police stations in London and Kent 1984-86, Edwards (1989) established that front line officers saw domestic disputes as low status, boring and frustrating work. Although many situations contained the potential of violence escalating after police left, the police still showed unwillingness to act. In this study, the only type of situation which led to arrest was one in which the violence continued after the police arrived on the scene or where the assailant was directly aggressive towards the police. Edwards (1989) concluded that the use of police discretion in dealing with marital violence leads to under-enforcement of the law.

Police recording practices have also made it difficult to track the incidence of domestic violence or the action taken in response to calls for assistance (Edwards 1989; Smith 1989). In Edwards' study, it was shown that calls were not recorded in station message books, that some were recorded inaccurately and that some were marked NCPA (no call for police action). This also happened even where considerable time had been spent at the scene. The general tendency was towards 'no criming' or 'criming down' of incidents.

The Effect Of Police Policy Changes In Britain

In Great Britain, contrary to the situation in the United States, no policy or practice of mandatory arrest for domestic violence assaults exists: arrest is at the discretion of the police officer attending the incident. However, in July 1990, following policy changes in the Metropolitan and West Yorkshire police forces, the Home Office published Circular 60/1990, which recommended that police forces develop policy statements and strategies which recognise domestic violence as a crime. It underlined the duty of the police to protect the victim and to take punitive action against the assailant. By 1991, in response to the Home Office recommendations, all forces in the United Kingdom had formulated policy statements on domestic violence.

What has been the effect of these police policies on the treatment of domestic violence incidents? The policy is too new to have been extensively researched but the recently published Home Office

study on the impact of Circular 60/1990 on both policy and practice (Grace 1995) and some other studies give an indication of progress in this field.

The Home Office study, published five years after the 1990 Circular, was based on a telephone survey of 42 of the 43 police forces in England and Wales and a more detailed study of five police forces in England, as well as interviews with victims and other agencies. It found evidence that officers in general had increased their awareness of domestic violence issues and showed greater understanding and sympathy for victims. However, one third of operational officers had not heard of Circular 60/1990 and half stated that they had not received any new guidelines on domestic violence, although their managers considered that the information had been disseminated. Officers attending incidents were aware that arrest should be a priority but they were influenced by their own perceptions of whether the complainant would support an arrest or prosecution.

Acknowledging the difficulties for police officers in the field, the report noted the tendency amongst the police to arrest domestic violence offenders for breach of the peace, possibly since this offence does not require complainant evidence. Officers sometimes described how breach of the peace charges were brought even in very violent circumstances, where it would appear that it would be more appropriate for the police to utilise the Offences Against the Person Act (1861). Consequently the report recommends that police officers should give more consideration to arrest on charges of assault rather than breaches of the peace. It also calls for more efficient practices to record and monitor domestic violence: in the study, only a quarter of operational officers reported being able consistently to check police records for a previous history of assaults before attending an incident. West Midlands Police force is commended for its method of coding domestic violence cases separately on its computerised Command and Control system. On the issue of officer training, the report advises the police to take up offers of training assistance from other agencies.

Alongside the Home Office study, other academic researchers have also gathered data on current police practice in relation to domestic violence. Mooney (1993) noted in a North London survey that women who had sought police help recently were generally pleased with their treatment particularly if they had been in contact with

one of the new Domestic Violence Units, the functions of which are outlined below. In an update of her earlier work, Edwards (1989) compared the situation before and after the Metropolitan Police Force Order of 1987 by analysing statistics in two London divisions. During the period, incidents logged at the station increased by 77 per cent, incidents recorded as crimes increased from 12 per cent to 21 per cent, incidents resulting in arrests increased from 2 per cent to 17 per cent and crimes that were 'no crimed' decreased from 83 per cent to 64 per cent. Metropolitan Police statistics for London as a whole show that recorded domestic violence increased dramatically from 770 incidents in 1985 to 9800 in 1992, the latter figure representing 26 per cent of all recorded assaults in London (Morley and Mullender 1994). Clearly one of the main advantages of having a Force Order on domestic violence is that it leads to improved data collection but the variation in recording systems between police forces has also led to difficulties of comparability.

Various studies also give an indication of arrest rates for domestic violence incidents in different parts of the United Kingdom. The Home Office Study (1995) notes that the rate for the West Midlands is 12 per cent for all recorded cases of domestic violence and for the Thames Valley, the figure is 14 per cent.

One of the few forces to undertake regular evaluations is West Yorkshire. From 1990 they have been carrying out annual surveys of domestic violence, the data from which enables them to put domestic violence 'at the forefront of (their) priorities' (West Yorkshire Police 1993). Officers are required to complete a form after every incident and enter the information in a Domestic Violence Index at the station. The surveys detail:

- incidence, time, repeat calls, details of age, sex and relationship of victim and assailant;

- police action, including advice given, arrest, charge, custody and time in custody;

- time taken to respond to calls.

The surveys point to a general overall improvement in police performance, although the 1993 report expressed concern regarding a slight decline in the proportion of arrests (24.2 per cent in 1993), while noting that police officers continued to make enquiries to trace offenders who had left the scene. The 1993 survey report

claims that a slight decrease in repeat incidents indicates that 'assailants would appear to be getting the message that their behaviour will not be tolerated'. However, in 1993, there was only a 50 per cent arrest rate where actual injunctions were in force; this is described as a disappointing deterioration in positive action. A further weak area in performance was the decrease in referrals to Women's Aid from the Force's own Domestic Violence and Child Protection Unit. On the positive side, an improvement in police response time to calls for assistance was noted, as was the increased length of time assailants were held in custody indicating, the report suggests, a stronger commitment to the force policy and 'a determination by the police to ensure women and children are protected and not left at continuing risk'.

In contrast to the improved performance claimed for the West Yorkshire police, a study by Smith (1994) found a change of policy but little change in practice in the Cheshire police. Although key elements of the Home Office Circular had been adopted into force policy, there was a divergence between police managers who, as a group, considered domestic violence to be an important policing issue, and police in operational practice. Smith found a low incidence of perpetrators being arrested (in only 43 per cent of cases where injunctions with power of arrest existed) and a high incidence of 'exit' from the police system (records marked No Further Action or No Complaints Made). In the vast majority of cases, police did not take positive action. Concerning the safety and welfare of victims, in most cases the victims reported that police did not ask if they needed, or arrange for them to receive, medical treatment and did not take them to a place of safety or assist with alternative arrangements. This is a highly critical assessment and leads Smith to conclude that 'Whilst most police profess to support force policy, the reality of practice reveals a facade' (Smith 1994).

Domestic Violence Units

An innovation in the wake of police policy changes in Britain has been the creation of special Domestic Violence Units, the first of which was established in Tottenham, London in 1987. The Home Office study (Grace 1995) found that while only five of the police forces in England and Wales had units dedicated solely to domestic violence, half had specialist units with some responsibilities for this offence and most had at least a Domestic Violence Liaison Officer.

Twenty-four officers with special responsibility for domestic violence (Domestic Violence Officers) were interviewed for the Home Office study. The report found that these Officers were very committed to their work and offered long term support to victims. Domestic Violence Officers see the care and protection of victims as their main function whilst arrest or prosecution is not a priority for them. Victims were very positive about their contact with the Officers while reporting more mixed experiences of uniformed police. The report states that the availability of Domestic Violence Officers, above all factors, ensures that victims are satisfied with their treatment by the police. The Domestic Violence Officers have also developed good working relationships with other agencies.

On the other hand, the Home Office study found that Domestic Violence Officers were often overworked and burdened with laborious recording and referral systems. They were frequently marginalised and not kept fully informed of domestic violence incidents in their area and therefore had a limited impact on the generalist police response to domestic violence. Those who worked within Family Protection Units felt their work had a lower priority than child protection.

Morley and Mullender (1994) state that there is some evidence that police divisions with Domestic Violence Units do better than those without, in terms of arrest rate, number of written incident reports, referrals to the Crown Prosecution Service, victim confidence and inter-agency work. However, they describe the lack of a systematic approach to Domestic Violence Units within most forces or between forces as a major concern. Domestic Violence Units' roles differ from unit to unit, as do their relations with 'mainstream' policing, their lines of support and their accountability.

A major new study of the Domestic Violence Unit which is the cornerstone of the South Tyneside Domestic Violence Initiative (Walker and McNicol 1994) gives a detailed focus on some of these concerns. The researchers based their report on an analysis of referrals and police incident logs, on an observational study of the day-to-day work of the Domestic Violence Unit and on interviews with victims. They found that the unit had much to be proud of but serious questions emerged about the rather ambivalent role of Domestic Violence Unit Officers, who did not get involved in 'policing' domestic violence but spent most of their time attempting to

make contact with and listening to victims. The researchers queried the amount of time the officers spent on administrative tasks and the unwieldy system which resulted in a majority of victims never actually receiving help. They suggest that the Domestic Violence Unit's remit of support and specialist advice could be enacted more effectively if it was staffed by civilian professionals. The initiative had also failed to reduce the number of repeat calls. Walker and McNicol found a 'worrying lack of understanding' of the Domestic Violence Initiative amongst officers and about the role of the Domestic Violence Unit, with the result that it was in danger of becoming isolated and marginalised.

Much of the literature on criminal justice system intervention focuses on policing; fewer studies deal with prosecution, the courts and sentencing. Smith (1989) has denoted this as 'a relatively neglected area'. It is to this neglected area of research that we now turn.

Prosecution

A major criticism in the research on the policing of domestic violence, particularly in the United States, is that arrest is isolated as one factor in preventing domestic violence while in reality the situation requires consideration of the varying outcomes of arrest including the effect of co-ordinating various aspects of the criminal justice system, preferably in alliance with community helping agencies. First, we comment on issues relating to prosecution and draw on evidence from both the United States and the United Kingdom. Initially there is some distinction by country but in the main the evidence here is combined. Ford and Regoli (1993) claim that we know very little about the effectiveness of prosecution policies in preventing violence. Nevertheless, Cahn and Lerman (1991) argue that prosecution should be a priority for three reasons:

1. Prosecution is 'the formal expression of social norms'. If abusers are not prosecuted, they have tacit permission to continue.

2. Unless arrest is followed by prosecution, law enforcement is 'a fiction', since only the prosecutor and judge may exercise continuing authority over a defendant following arrest.

3. Violence against women is often serious and usually chronic. As victim and offender commonly live together, it is a

particularly dangerous form of violent crime and one which, without intervention, is likely to continue.

Evidence From the United States on Factors Influencing Decisions to Prosecute

Several American studies have touched on the question of what happens after arrest. In the Minneapolis study, only three of 136 suspects arrested were fined or imprisoned; at Milwaukee there were virtually no prosecutions; at Charlotte, only 35 per cent of suspects listed for prosecution were in fact prosecuted; at Omaha, however, 64 per cent of those arrested were later sentenced (Ford and Regoli 1993). These figures highlight the variation in prosecution in the various jurisdictions.

A large scale study in Canada (McLeod 1983) found that those cases which are prosecuted, are frequently downgraded, for example treated as a misdemeanour rather than a felony which is a much more serious offence. A National Crime Survey in the United States showed that one-third of misdemeanour domestic violence cases would have been treated as felonies if committed by strangers (Buzawa and Buzawa 1990).

Elliott (1989) found that regardless of the type of crime, cases are less likely to be prosecuted when the offender is known to the victim and when prosecuted, are more likely to result in acquittal. More prosecutions result where defendants have 'negative' attributes (alcohol and drug abuse problems, failure to comply with police) whereas 'negative' victim attributes (poor parenting skills, substance abuse) reduce the chance of prosecution.

Evidence From Great Britain on Factors Influencing Decisions to Prosecute

Most of the British studies agree that a key factor determining whether prosecution would proceed in cases of domestic violence was the presence of a public disorder element, especially if the police themselves were challenged. 'When violence is prosecuted, it is to secure order and police authority rather than to satisfy the victim' (Sanders, 1987). In addition, it may be easier to secure a conviction in such cases. Edwards (1986) established that a mere 17 out of her sample of 773 domestic violence incidents reported to the police were finally proceeded with. In Britain, as in the United States, there is downgrading of offences (Grace 1995). The Home Office study reports that

police officers were more likely to use the charge of Breach of the Peace since complainant evidence was unnecessary but where charges of GBH or AOABH may be more appropriate.

Wasoff (1982), in her research into Scottish courts, also found that domestic violence cases were more likely than non-domestic violence cases to be assigned to lower district courts. Since these courts have more limited sanctions, Wasoff adduces this to be evidence that domestic violence cases are being treated less seriously. Sanders (1987) produced a different explanation in his study of prosecution decision making in three English police force areas. He argued that male victims are more protected by the criminal justice system than are women. While agreeing that there is a gender bias in the courts, he argued that it is not a product of sexist attitudes, but of a structural bias in the law itself against the prosecution of personal violence: there is a disregard of the wishes of victims of both domestic and non-domestic violence. However, it could also be argued that the structural bias to which he refers reflects how sexist attitudes can become frozen into institutional structures where they remain unchallenged.

Smith (1989) and Hart (1993), reviewing the literature on factors influencing both police decisions on the 'criming' of domestic violence and the decision to prosecute, point to some of the attitudes and beliefs which are commonly held by the decision-makers. These are:

- that domestic violence offences are trivial and the victim 'undeserving';
- that it is a private matter in which they should not intervene;
- that domestic violence victims are unreliable witnesses who withdraw complaints and fail to cooperate with police and prosecutors.

Victim Co-operation and Prosecution

One of the most contentious issues in relation to policing and prosecution in this field is the extent to which victims withdraw their evidence. Lorna Smith notes that the research evidence on this is contradictory. Faragher (1985) reports a one in ten withdrawal; Dobash and Dobash (1979) found a 6 per cent withdrawal and Wasoff (1982) reported only one request to withdraw (which was refused) out of 59 cases. Yet in Edwards' (1986) study of inci-

dents for which police made out crime reports, almost all of the four-fifths which were later 'no crimed' were on the grounds of complainant withdrawal. Sanders (1987) points out that withdrawals of complaints can also be made by victims of non-domestic violence, but after the decision to prosecute was made domestic violence victims in his study were less likely to withdraw than non-domestic violence victims. Nevertheless, in the latter case, the police were more likely to proceed with the case anyway, despite reservations about the 'reliability' of the witness.

Ford and Regoli (1993) argue that the common belief that women withdraw cases because of reconciliation with defendants is not typically the reason for terminating a case. However, this view is also contested by police officers as well as by those operating within the judicial system. It remains a problem for further research. Interestingly, an important finding from these studies is that in some cases, initiation of charges alone may bring about an improvement in defendant behaviour (Ford 1995).

Ferraro and Boychulk (1992) claim that the proportion of cases dropped from prosecution in the United States as a result of the inadequacy of police reports in documentary evidence (10 per cent) is nearly as great as prosecutions dropped because of victim reluctance or refusal to give evidence (13 per cent). In relation to policing, then, issues arise for not only improved police recording mechanisms, as noted earlier, but also for creating a better system for documenting evidence in cases of domestic violence. If these are in place then the likelihood of a successful prosecution is increased.

In the Home Office study, Grace (1995) reports on interviews with victims which suggest that providing the support of a Domestic Violence Officer may encourage more women to pursue a prosecution. The Crown Prosecution Service respondents in this study emphasised that evidence in domestic violence cases must be of 'a very high quality' to ensure a conviction. But the author also points out that Section 23 of the Criminal Justice Act (1988) allows written evidence in court if victims feel intimidated, though this is rarely used in practice.

A further crucial factor in successful prosecution may be the timing of arrest and subsequent prosecution. Evason (1982), commenting on a 1976 study of the Bedfordshire police which showed that only 18 out of 104 wife assault cases were withdrawn, notes that the police made

21

a practice of arresting assailants and bringing them before the courts without delay. In reality, this is much more likely to happen for Breach of the Peace offences than for charges prosecuted under the offences Against the Person Act. Evason states that she is not surprised by difficulties in securing prosecution in these circumstances: 'a change of heart is naturally likely to occur if a woman is left in a house with her assailant immediately after an assault has occurred and has to remain in the house with him during the lengthy period that may elapse before a case comes to court' (Evason 1982).

There may also be a discordance between police attitudes and victim wishes. Smith (1994), as already noted, found that the traditional police paradigm of 'the reluctant victim' continued to prevail operationally in the Cheshire police, despite policy changes at police management level. While 80 per cent of the victims in his sample had suffered criminal injuries and 63 per cent stated that they wanted the perpetrator prosecuted, only 52 per cent were actually asked by the police if they wished to prosecute, police behaviour thus providing a self-fulfilling prophecy that the majority of victims do not support prosecution. One quarter of victims considered that the police persuaded them not to prosecute and 48 per cent were not asked to make a written statement, though almost all who were asked did so. In Montgomery and Bell's Northern Ireland study (1986) the police took no action in the majority of incidents, yet 67 per cent of the women said that they would have been willing to give evidence in court.

'No-Drop' Policies And The Compellability Of Witnesses

In relation to prosecution, controversy exists around the issue of 'no-drop' policies in North America where cases are pursued even against the wishes of the victim. Similar controversy in the United Kingdom has surrounded the issue of compellability of witnesses, since the Police and Criminal Evidence Act 1984 can oblige victims to give evidence against their partners. One particular case which created a good deal of controversy in England centred on a woman who was jailed for contempt of court after failing to give evidence after threats by her assailant.

Dobash and Dobash (1992) report that the Duluth project abandoned a 'no-drop' policy because of reservations about its impact on victims; conviction rates thereafter dropped to less than 50 per cent

(Pence 1989). On the other hand, Morley and Mullender (1992) point to the claim that if the decision to arrest and charge is left to the victim, she can be in practice controlled by the assailant, who has power to intimidate her. The report on domestic violence by Victim Support (1992) recommends that if domestic violence is to be treated as seriously as other crimes of violence it may be necessary to compel victims to give evidence but 'it is against natural justice to compel a witness who is thereby endangered without offering protection and support'.

Reporting on the findings of his Indianapolis Domestic Violence Prosecution Experiment, Ford (1995) declares that whether a man is prosecuted under policies leading to harsh punishment or rehabilitation is irrelevant: what matters is that he faces prosecution. The surprise finding of this research is that permitting victims to drop charges significantly reduces the risk of further violence (in cases where victims themselves had filed charges). Ford argues that this is empowering to women because a woman in offering to drop prosecution can bargain for her security with her attacker and also by securing more powerful allies in criminal justice system personnel, she can threaten to invoke their power to deter her abuser: 'the warrant for arrest signifies their attentiveness to her grievance'. Ford asserts that 'no-drop' policies actually disempower and further jeopardize women. Arguing for a coordinated criminal justice system response, he states that:

'... while trying to address the problem of wife battering on a more global scale, the prosecutor's interest in redressing a crime against the state must not displace the goal of stopping violence against individual battered women' (Ford 1995:8).

This point is reiterated by Barron (1990) when she stresses that if prosecution is undertaken, the interests of the woman and her children and in particular their safety (especially where the couple continue to live in the same house) should be paramount; the woman's wishes regarding proceeding with prosecution should always be heeded. The priority of victim preference regarding arrest and prosecution is also supported by Buzawa and Buzawa (1993).

Victim Confidence

Discussing criminal justice system intervention in general, Morley and Mullender (1992) state that for a woman it may mean a transfer

of control from the private realm (that of an individual male batterer) to the public (a largely male coercive institution). For these authors, both may be experienced as abusive. The issue revolves around how control of the outcome of intervention by police and prosecutors can be handled in a way that is empowering to the victim. It is clear that many women have little confidence that the judicial system can both redress their grievances and protect them. When serious assaults are downgraded, when prosecution is delayed, when women are not offered protection from further violence, they 'may conclude that the costs and risks of prosecution outweigh the potential consequences for assailants' (Hart 1993). The reality of factors such as fear of increased violence, economic ruin for the family, unsympathetic attitudes of lawyers and judges and intimidation by the court process itself (Barron 1990; Victim Support 1992; McWilliams and McKiernan 1993) cannot be discounted, hence the importance of victim advocacy and support programmes, victim compensation and 'sentences that clearly call batterers to account and safeguard victims' (Hart 1993).

Sentencing

Only a limited amount of research exists into court sentencing for domestic violence offences but from what is available it would appear that Hart's criteria above are not being met. Jaffe et al. (1986) noted that in Canada, police decisions regarding arrest may be affected by a perceived lack of support in the courts, where cases are dismissed or given light sentences. Wasoff (1982) found that domestic violence cases as a group attracted lower fines and shorter prison sentences than non-domestic violence cases, fining being the most common disposal (three-quarters of cases). Imprisonment was the least frequent disposal (6 per cent). Dobash and Dobash in their 1974 Glasgow research revealed that nearly 25 per cent of wife assaulters were merely told off by magistrates, 58 per cent were given a small fine, 3.4 per cent were put on probation and 12 per cent were imprisoned.

Edwards (1986) analysed sentencing practice in the few cases prosecuted in her 1984-85 London policing study. Of the 16 cases, only nine were finally formally sentenced. Of the cases heard in the Magistrates Courts, disposals were fines ranging from £40 to £75 and a suspended prison sentence. Three of the more serious cases were heard at the Crown Court: one defendant was acquitted, one

received a nine month prison sentence and another a nine month suspended prison sentence for wounding. Edwards (1986:229) argues that counsel 'frequently invoke gender-based ideologies as rationales for explaining and excusing male violence', minimizing the criminality and dangerousness of the crime by reference to the domestic context. She cites an appeal case where counsel has described the client as 'not a person from whom society needs to be protected': he had struck and blinded his wife with a hammer.

In Montgomery and Bell's (1986) Northern Ireland study, charges were laid in only eight cases out of 62 incidents. In two cases, the women dropped the charges of Grievous Bodily Harm: in one case the woman was advised to do so by the police, in the other she acted to spare her child from having to give evidence in court against her father. Of the six cases that came to court, police brought charges in two instances of child assault alone, although the wives had also been assaulted and these offenders were given suspended prison sentences (plus a fine of £200 in one case). Sentencing for the remaining cases included a suspended sentence for GBH, quashed on appeal; probation and a fine for assault; three months imprisonment for GBH (for which the man served six weeks). In this latter case, the man was released after being charged and attacked his ex-wife five times before the case came to court three months later. A later assault resulted in another one month prison sentence, but this woman continued to live in fear of attack. She was 'sickened' by the leniency of sentencing and all the victims expressed dissatisfaction with this aspect of the judicial process. Montgomery and Bell recommended that the Lord Chief Justice should issue guidelines to judges and magistrates on the suitability of sentences for wife assault offenders.

The issue of whether more punitive sentencing and, in particular, imprisonment is effective in deterring domestic violence is of course a contentious one. Barron (1990) states that imprisonment is unlikely to be the final solution to the problem for the woman since on release, some men may seek vengeance and continue their violent behaviour although others may be 'brought up short' by the sentence. It may be an effective remedy in some cases, but the effectiveness is 'very limited and conditional'. Hague and Malos (1993) are also concerned about the implications for women after a man is released from prison; in their opinion, Home Office advice that the women should be informed of an imminent release only deals with part of the problem. Nevertheless, they conclude that it is

important that the offence is not trivialized by being treated more leniently than other equally serious offences.

Craig (1992), herself a magistrate, considers the sentencing dilemma for the magistrate. She predicts that Magistrates Courts will see increasing numbers of domestic violence cases in the years ahead as younger women are 'more ready to fight for their rights' and as police prosecution policies become more established. She notes that younger, co-habiting women are more likely to report domestic violence and to expect custodial sentences for offenders. She recognises the ambivalence of older more dependent women with children, an ambivalence sometimes shared by the magistrate who 'will be concerned for the integrity of the family and about the economic and social consequences of sending a breadwinner to jail'. Magistrates too fear that imprisonment may increase the aggressiveness and vindictiveness of the offender on release; on the other hand, a heavy fine may only impose additional suffering on families and is unrealistic for an unemployed defendant. Another problem for magistrates is the judicial principle that an offender should be sentenced for his present crime, which principle must be set against the assessment of risk where there is a pattern of violence rather than a 'solitary and untypical' offence: in the former case, Craig states that maximum prison sentences must be considered. In other cases, a short immediate sentence may serve the functions of bringing relief to victims, avoiding the institutionalization of longer sentencing and 'sending a clear message to the public that courts will condemn and punish wife battering'.

Other Disposals: Adult Cautioning

Another method of dealing with domestic violence offenders is by adult cautioning. Buchan and Edwards (1991) researched the effectiveness of deferred cautioning at Streatham for cases of domestic assault involving minor injury. Most victims expressed satisfaction with the procedure, with 88 per cent of offenders not coming to the attention of the police again during the monitoring period, 28 per cent stating that the process of arrest and deferred cautioning made them alter their behaviour. The new procedure was widely accepted by police officers themselves and by the public who reported double the number of domestic violence incidents to the police after the first year of the project. The research suggested that charging an offender is no more of a deterrent than cautioning but cautioning

seemed to find favour with most victims, 75 per cent of whom agreed with arrest but 52 per cent of whom said they would not give evidence in court following police charging of the assailant.

In Northern Ireland, Mercer (1993) found that his Domestic Violence Liaison Inspector respondents were strongly in favour of extending adult cautioning to domestic violence cases, pointing out that as an alternative to issuing charges which require a court hearing, it would obviate the problem of victims withdrawing charges at court. He describes it as a more powerful tool than the informal advice and warning used by police in 13 to 15 per cent of domestic violence cases. His reasoning here is that adult cautioning is recorded in police records and should pose more of a threat to offenders than verbal warnings.

A Coordinated Criminal Justice Response

Although police response to domestic violence offenders has been a major focus for research in this field, researchers also point to the inadequacy of such an approach which ignores a concerted police response involving prosecution, sentencing of the offender and support for the victim. Concentrating on policing alone is akin to looking for a short term solution only and may hark back to the reluctance to treat domestic violence seriously. Morley and Mullender (1992) report that there is a growing awareness in the USA and Canada that arrest/charge alone is not enough: 'Many jurisdictions are moving towards a criminal justice response which is both internally co-ordinated (between police, prosecution and sentencing) and integrated within a broader community response to provide women with a comprehensive support system'. It is these jurisdictions which report having achieved positive results with arrest.

Below we provide examples from North America of two co-ordinated community responses to domestic violence which also provide support for the victim. As such they constitute examples of good practice in this field.

London, Ontario

This initiative was based on the premise that the criminal justice system should take the lead within an integrated community response. The police brought charges in all cases of domestic violence where it was believed an offence had occurred (thus shifting the responsibility

of laying charges from victims to the police). This resulted in a 2500 per cent increase in police charges between 1979-83 (Jaffe et al. 1986). There was evidence of victim satisfaction (56 per cent dissatisfaction before the pro-change policy; 5.5 per cent dissatisfaction after) and of decreased violence and fewer repeat calls. A co-ordinating committee introduced a treatment programme for offenders, attendance at which can be ordered by the court; a victim advocacy service; community publicity and educational campaigns; and good provision of shelters and alternative housing for victims.

Duluth Abuse Intervention Project (DAIP)

This project in Duluth, Minnesota, began in 1980 and is described by Dobash and Dobash (1992:180) as 'the most successful justice project in the United States'. A programme of police training combined with a pro-arrest policy was introduced. Officers were required to justify decisions in written reports when they did not arrest. This led to more arrests being made which in turn led to a reduction in assaults as well as a 47 per cent reduction in repeat calls (1982-84). The distinctiveness of this project was that it laid stress on prosecution, with a marked increased in domestic violence cases being pursued through the courts. In 1980, 29 per cent of cases resulted in a conviction; by 1983, the figure was 87 per cent. Pence (1989) attributes this to several factors such as the adoption of prosecution guidelines which discourage charge dismissal and the use of advocates to work with women throughout the court process. On conviction, an offender may be sentenced to imprisonment; or to probation or a suspended prison sentence, with required attendance at a batterers' programme. Ferraro (1995) holds that this model 'increases accountability and an integrated response from the entire system'. One would also think that the training of judges and magistrates is a significant element of a coordinated response, particularly for those tasked with the responsibility of making decisions about sending offenders to prison or diverting them to a programme for abusers. The literature, however, pays minimal attention to the issue of training.

Civil Law

Great Britain

As a result of the legislation of the 1970s in Britain (see page 12), it became possible for a victim of domestic violence to obtain an

injunction to prevent a husband from molesting his wife and children and to exclude him from the matrimonial home. This protection was later extended to co-habitees. Previously the only relief had been through an interlocutory order, obtained as part of divorce or separation proceedings. The law made provision for attaching a power of arrest without warrant for breach of these injunctions. In the United States, nearly all states have civil injunction legislation of this kind.

Reviewing the operation of the legislation in both the United States and Britain, Dobash and Dobash (1992) state that evidence from three studies in the United States shows the effectiveness of the measures. In one study in four states, 72 per cent of victims surveyed found injunctions effective and 42 per cent found them very effective. However, in Britain, these researchers note the reluctance and hesitancy of Scottish courts where very few exclusion orders were granted in the two years after the legislation was introduced. Judicial attitudes to the use of the new orders was perhaps summed up by the English judge who said: 'I find it difficult to believe that it could ever be fair, save in most exceptional circumstances, to keep a man out of his flat or house for more than a few months' (cited in Dobash and Dobash 1992).

Although there has been an increase in the use of injunctions, a Women's Aid Federation (England) survey in 1981 found that only 50 per cent of injunctions included an exclusion order. In 1987, while over 15,000 injunctions were granted in England and Wales, only 28 per cent had a power of arrest attached. There is considerable regional variation in the use of powers of arrest and exclusion orders and a judicial reluctance to imprison the offender should a breach of the order occur. Furthermore, orders are ineffective if police do not know of their existence or do not enforce powers of arrest (Faragher 1985). Binney et al. (1981) interviewed 35 women who had obtained an injunction, of whom 17 had called the police because of violence. Only four out of 17 assailants were charged with breach of the injunction, even though ten of the women had been seriously injured.

Barron (1990) in her study of the effectiveness of legal protection for women and children experiencing domestic violence recommended, in relation to the enforcement of injunctions, that:

• powers of arrest should be added as a general rule where the offence of Actual Bodily Harm has occurred;

- that it should be the norm for police to arrest for breach of an order and

- that the assailant should be brought back to court, even if he is a first offender, and treated severely, as a deterrent to himself and others.

She also noted that exclusion orders were almost never granted *ex parte* and recommended that the application should be heard without delay. Barron criticized the practice common in the County Court of accepting a sworn undertaking from the aggressor, in place of a court order. She argues that the former is more likely to be disregarded, not only by the offender but by the police and courts. On the other hand, solicitors interviewed for recent research in Hull (Kewley, Cromack *et al.* 1994) regarded such undertakings as 'often a satisfactory mechanism'. Clearly there is a contradiction in what the solicitors in Hull report and the conclusions of Barron's wider survey of women's experience of the court system. Sworn undertakings do not exist in Northern Ireland. Since they do not have the same legal force in practice as court orders, there may be some concern if these were to be introduced by the proposed legislation on Family Law.

Northern Ireland

In Northern Ireland, there are some differences in the way in which the legislation operates. Article 18 of the Domestic Proceedings (NI) Order 1980 contained provision for spouses to apply for Personal Protection and Exclusion Orders, extended to co-habitees by the Family Law (Miscellaneous Provisions (NI) Order 1984). While it appears that in England applications for injunctions are commonly held in the County Court (Kewley, Cromack *et al.* 1994; Barron 1990), most in Northern Ireland are heard in the Magistrates Courts where interim or emergency orders can be expeditiously granted where necessary for a five-week period pending a full hearing. In theory, emergency orders can be granted within 24 hours. The research undertaken by Montgomery and Bell (1986) found that 58 per cent of the women they interviewed were able to obtain orders in less than a week. They are not effective until served personally on the respondent by the RUC or a summons server. Personal Protection Orders can be granted with no expiry date but are often made for a fixed term such as two years. Exclusion Orders

cannot exceed six months which means that a victim has to apply for a renewal of the order, if needed (Quinn 1991).

In the case of a breach of an order, police in Northern Ireland, unlike their English counterparts, have the discretionary power to arrest without a warrant. However, confusion followed a judgement by Judge Petrie at the County Court in 1991 (later upheld in the Appeal Court), which for a period affected prosecution of breaches of Personal Protection Orders and Exclusion Orders, by placing the onus to prosecute on the victim herself rather than on the police.

Evason, writing in 1982 when the legislation in Northern Ireland was still very recent, noted that the effectiveness of the new provisions would depend on the attitude of the police and their willingness to take prompt action when an order is breached. The research at that time suggested that 'unless police attitudes change drastically the new legislation has little chance of success' (Evason 1982). So has Evason's pessimistic forecast been borne out in practice? Research evidence is limited to two studies (Montgomery and Bell 1986; McWilliams and McKiernan 1993) and is reported on below but Brown's 1986 pilot study in Magistrates Courts certainly suggested that victims were making use of the legislation: applications for personal protection orders and exclusion orders were the second most common form of application in family law cases (36.5 per cent of 600 applications).

Effectiveness of the Orders in Northern Ireland

Montgomery and Bell (1986) found a lack of knowledge of the existence and applicability of protection orders amongst those women in their sample who did not have orders. However, 33 women out of their sample of 67 had been granted personal protection orders and/ or exclusion orders on one or more occasions. Of these

- 40 per cent reported a deterrent effect;

- 17 per cent stated that the violence escalated;

- 40 per cent claimed that the orders made no difference (because the man was not afraid of the police).

In relation to breaches of the orders, of the 40 per cent who had called the police at the time of the breach, the following outcomes were noted:

- in 31 per cent of these cases, no action was taken;

- in only 7 per cent of cases were the assailants arrested and charged;

- the rest (62 per cent) were warned, removed, removed and held overnight or had left the scene.

It should however be noted that these researchers stated that their sample may be under-representative of women who have found protection orders effective.

Over half (56 per cent) of the women interviewed in McWilliams and McKiernan's 1993 study of domestic violence in Northern Ireland had personal protection and exclusion orders but only one quarter found them to be useful. Problems reported by the women included difficulties in serving the orders, orders being ignored by partners or not enforced by police and courts. Some found that the court response to the breach of an order was only a small fine or a reprimand. Concern was expressed about the order's application to the marital home only whereas women felt endangered in other locations also. Some women needed to move to a secret address to escape the violence: in these cases, fear of being found was a reason not to seek an exclusion order, as the order would have revealed their address. This has been a difficult problem which has, as yet, not been resolved since not to state the details of the victim's address raises issues of civil liberties in relation to the respondent's movements.

Logue (1989) called for more research into the effectiveness of civil remedies and police response using more representative sampling of the population of victims who have obtained Personal Protection and Exclusion Orders in Northern Ireland. Apart from useful evidence from the two studies cited above, such a large-scale study on this specific topic has yet to be undertaken.

Conclusion

Much of the literature in both the United Kingdom and the United States has focused on the police response to domestic violence with much less attention being paid to prosecution and sentencing. The literature has been highly critical of the police response both in relation to organisational issues (such as inadequate information

systems, poor training, limitations on powers of arrest, poor documentary evidence for prosecution) and police attitudes towards intervention on domestic violence. The police response in general has been criticised for failing to acknowledge the dynamics of domestic violence and for treating each case as a single incident rather than as a process which can have serious and life threatening consequences.

There remains an ongoing debate about the deterrent effects of mandatory arrest given the inconsistent results of the Minneapolis domestic violence experiment and its various replications in the United States. The general consensus seems to be that arrest without serious follow up and in isolation from other sanctions has limited effect. The literature points to the need for greater integration between the policing and judicial system, a clear follow through and greater liaison with agencies tasked with providing victims with comprehensive support particularly when decisions have been taken to arrest, charge and prosecute. A model to follow here would be the Duluth Abuse Intervention Project.

The situation in Britain is very different. The emphasis is still on police discretion in cases of domestic violence and much attention has been paid to the under enforcement of the law in this area. Although specific Force Orders have been drawn up, the few evaluations which have been undertaken point to a change of policy rather than of practice. Recently however, there is clear evidence of more specialist attention being paid to domestic violence by police officers, particularly where Domestic Violence Units have taken on an investigative role in relation to prosecution. However, there is still concern over the methods used to record data and about the fact that even where injunctions are in place, the evidence for arrest varies throughout the United Kingdom. There appears to be a divergence between police managers who, as a group, consider domestic violence to be an important policing issue and operational practice where officers on the ground apply policy inconsistently and without the efficiency, uniformity or professionalism aspired to in policy statements.

The provision of specialist officers who are able to respond to the needs of victims, through dedicated Domestic Violence Units, does appear to make some difference to successful prosecutions. Concern has been expressed, however, about the work overload and

marginalisation of officers within these units and about clarification of their functions. To date, no decision has been taken in Northern Ireland to establish Domestic Violence Units.

Research material on prosecutions for domestic violence is extremely limited. What is available points to downgrading of charges and leniency in sentencing. When serious assaults are downgraded, when prosecution is delayed, when women are not offered protection from further violence, they 'may conclude that the costs and risks of prosecution outweigh the potential consequences for assailants' (Hart 1993). This may indeed be one of the reasons for an apparent higher withdrawal rate in domestic violence cases, though the extent to which women withdraw from prosecutions is a point on which researchers are currently divided. A further contentious issue is the compellability of witnesses where victims are reluctant to proceed with a prosecution. Although some may wish to give evidence in court, they may be fearful of the repercussions for themselves and their children. Clearly there is a duty on police to minimise fear and to understand that the victim's wishes should be placed within a context of victim support and victim safety. In the absence of this, victim cooperation with the prosecution system remains an important issue.

Even less research has been undertaken in the field of court sentencing for domestic violence offences. A perceived lack of support from the courts impacts on the decision making of a range of help providers. For example, police decisions regarding arrest may be affected and voluntary agencies such as Women's Aid may be reluctant to tell women to pursue prosecution if they remain unconvinced that batterers are called to account. Lower fines, case dismissals, lighter sentences and shorter prison sentences distinguish domestic violence cases from other criminal assaults. Minimising criminality and excusing male violence by reference to the domestic context creates victim dissatisfaction with the system.

The literature also points to the dilemmas for magistrates relating to the appropriateness of fines and of imprisonment. Fines are seen as being punitive since the offender may deduct these from income which is provided for the family's welfare. However this presumes that such redistribution takes place between husband and wives. In the case of domestic violence offenders this may be an erroneous assumption. Imprisonment can also impact negatively on the victim

since it can lead some men to seek vengeance and continue their violent behaviour on release. In addition, despite the fact that a message is conveyed to offenders by the sentence, the sentence by itself may not be enough.

An important issue raised by Craig (1992) is that the judicial principle that an offender should be sentenced for his present crime provides a difficulty for domestic violence cases since there is generally a pattern of violence rather than a solitary offence. Sentencing procedures thus need to reflect the pattern of re-offending.

An alternative to issuing charges which require a court prosecution is the system of adult cautioning. This type of cautioning is a more powerful tool than a verbal warning and creates an alternative to a court hearing in cases where victims are reluctant to give evidence. The caution, recorded in police files, may have a deterrent effect since subsequent behaviour is under observation and there is the possibility of stiffer penalties being instituted should reoffending occur.

Civil law also provides remedies for domestic violence and it is apparent that the legislation operates differently in Northern Ireland compared to Great Britain. A number of studies have included discussion on its effectiveness and although problems have been identified with personal protection and exclusion orders, they would appear to be granted more expeditiously in Northern Ireland than elsewhere.

Where victims are reluctant to press charges in criminal assault cases, the use of civil legislation provides some evidence that they have sought to protect themselves and their children from domestic violence. The fact that victims turn to the state for security and protection shows the importance of evaluating the effectiveness of these orders and in particular of the police response when these orders are breached. The answer to much of the controversy surrounding withdrawals from prosecutions may be to build victim confidence rather than to blame the victim. We appear to be some way towards this but not as far down the road as we might like.

Even in today's context, women need repeatedly

- to be confirmed in their view that domestic violence is not acceptable;

- to be helped to get an account in their own minds and on record of just what they have faced;

- to believe that the remedies work and the punishment fits and

- to have fear of reprisals effectively removed.

The extent to which this happens in practice will be taken up in the following chapters.

THREE

Homicides, Attempted Murders and Assaults by Partners or Former Partners in the Context of Domestic Violence in Northern Ireland

For the purposes of this study, court and police data for Northern Ireland were requested for all criminal offences such as homicides, attempted murder and serious assaults relating to domestic violence since the mid-1980s. To date, there have been very few studies using court data of this kind to determine the extent and seriousness of domestic violence (Dobash and Dobash 1979; Edwards 1989). As computerised information becomes increasingly available it should be possible to carry out more detailed analyses of domestic violence related crime between the various regions of the United Kingdom. Due to current restrictions on material of this kind, this study focuses mainly on Northern Ireland although some comparative information is also provided for the Republic of Ireland as well as two British police forces. The final part of this chapter presents a discussion on the verdicts and sentences for murder, manslaughter and attempted murder cases between 1989 and 1994.

We start here with the criminal statistics on offences against the person (including domestic violence). These have been produced by the RUC in a computerised form since 1987. However, practices in use for the recording of relationships meant that figures relating to domestic violence prior to 1990 were not necessarily accurate. Homicide data for 1990 to 1994 were provided whilst detailed information on serious assaults was provided from 1992 only.[1] Our analysis of annual trends in domestic violence related crime is therefore limited but we have, nonetheless, sufficient material to make some preliminary observations.

Based on crime reports, the 1990-1994 data file contains information on the sex, age and marital status of the victim and offender. It

---

1. Given the number of assaults involved, a manual search for this data between 1987 and 1992 would have been a very time-consuming exercise.

also provides information on the relationship between the victim and the offender, but the way in which this is categorised can be slightly problematic. For this study, we were able to gather information on registered marital relationships encompassing both cohabiting and separated (including divorced) couples. In cases of *de facto* (common-law) marital relationships, the method used by police officers to code dissolved unions has not been made explicit particularly in the case of 'ex-common-law' relationships. These *de facto* unions may sometimes be coded as 'friends' or 'acquaintances' rather than as former common-law husbands or common-law wives, and any such cases will have been excluded from our analyses. What we need is a more accurate picture of all homicides and assaults related to domestic violence as well as the exact nature of the relationship between the victim and the offender. Improved data recording mechanisms need to be developed to incorporate a more comprehensive and accurate system of categorising relationships in which the victim has been assaulted by someone with whom they are currently in a relationship or with whom they previously had an intimate relationship.

Homicides In Intimate Relationships

There are a number of ways to obtain a picture of the extent of the fatalities related to domestic violence incidents in a particular country. One is to show the annual number of domestic violence homicides per hundred thousand population in the country, in much the same way as the annual homicide rate is calculated. The numbers involved are too small to make this a meaningful calculation for domestic violence homicides. A better way to gauge the size of the problem can be gained from calculating the number of domestic violence related homicides proportionate to the number of married and cohabiting relationships in the country. Using what they called "a spousal homicide rate", Wilson and Daly (1994) calculated the average number of domestic violence homicides per hundred thousand couples in the population each year in Canada and arrived at a rate of 1.7 for the country.[2] To date there have been few attempts to calculate spousal homicide rates elsewhere, but using the 1991 Census data this rate was calculated for Northern Ireland. The

---

2. Wilson and Daly calculate the rate per million couples in Canada. This has been adapted here for its equivalency per hundred thousand couples.

Census records a figure of 298,269 married and cohabiting couples for Northern Ireland in 1991 (Compton 1995). From Table 1, we know that the average number of spousal homicides per year between 1990-1994 was 5.8, therefore Northern Ireland's spousal homicide rate is 1.9. It is worth noting that the rate for Northern Ireland is higher than the Canadian spousal homicide rate, although the considerable difference in population size between these two countries makes this comparison much less meaningful.[3]

The calculation most frequently referred to in the literature on domestic violence is the percentage of domestic violence homicides as a proportion of the total annual homicides in each country. This percentage highlights the extent to which domestic violence figures as part of the overall homicide problem. This is set out in the table below and, as we can see, it fluctuates from year to year. Table 1 also provides some comparative data on the number of domestic violence homicides in countries similar to Northern Ireland. The table refers only to those male and female homicides in which the police have charged a current or previous spouse or partner with murder or manslaughter and does not include other individuals who might have been killed in the incident.[4] The Republic of Ireland has been used as a comparator because it has not experienced political conflict to the same extent as Northern Ireland. The two English regions are chosen because of the availability of police homicide data and because of their similarity in population size to Northern Ireland.

In Northern Ireland, in the period between 1990-1994, approximately one-fifth (23 per cent) of all non-political homicide victims were killed by a current or former partner. This is a higher proportion than that recorded for the Republic of Ireland and Yorkshire, despite Northern Ireland's relatively smaller population.[5] Since the

---

3. Despite the variation in this rate across the Canadian provinces, it is significant that only three out of the 13 Canadian provinces have a spousal homicide rate higher than the figure recorded for Northern Ireland.

4. The definition of partner is a person with whom the victim has had a sexual relationship. It includes both common-law partners and boyfriends/girlfriends.

5. In Devon and Cornwall, the total number of homicides (76) between 1990 and 1994 is lower than that recorded for the other three regions. This may be partially explained by the higher proportion of retired people living in this region. Since the total number of homicides is lower than in the other three regions, the percentage of domestic violence related homicides over the five year period is slightly higher.

TABLE 3.1
Comparative Data on all Homicides and Homicides related to Domestic Violence:
Northern Ireland, Republic of Ireland, West Yorkshire, Devon and Cornwall, 1990–1994

Year	Northern Ireland (Population 1.6 million)			Republic of Ireland (Population 3.5 million)			West Yorkshire (Population 2.0 million)			Devon and Cornwall (Population 1.5 million)		
Year	Domestic Violence	Total Homicides (non-political)*	% of All Homicides Related to Domestic Violence	Domestic Violence	Total Homicides	% of All Homicides Related to Domestic Violence	Domestic Violence	Total Homicides	% of All Homicides Related to Domestic Violence	Domestic Violence	Total Homicides	% of All Homicides Related to Domestic Violence
1990	Nil	17	Nil	1	26	4%	11	42	26%	4	12	33%
1991	9	31	29%	2	30	7%	4	35	11%	8	18	44%
1992	9	30	30%	4	41	10%	5	33	15%	5	13	38%
1993	7	24	29%	2	28	7%	11	27	41%	5	16	31%
1994	4	26	15%	1	32	3%	4	27	15%	4	17	24%
Total	29	128	23%	10	157	6%	35	164	21%	26	76	26%

Source: Police Force Statistics, RUC, West Yorkshire, Devon and Cornwall and Garda Siochana Crime Branch, 1995.

* Murders and manslaughters not arising from the security situation.

social and demographic features are similar in the Republic of Ireland and Yorkshire, the comparative difference raises questions as to why Northern Ireland has more domestic violence homicides each year. Devon and Cornwall's population size is also similar to that of Northern Ireland but its population includes a larger number of elderly people which may explain why its total homicide figure is relatively small. This smaller total has to be borne in mind in interpreting the higher proportion of domestic violence related killings in this region.

Further work is needed to establish the cause of death so that we can check for any variations across the regions. From some preliminary work, it would appear that the proportion of deaths caused by shootings is higher in Northern Ireland than elsewhere.[6] The use of legally held firearms in some of these cases introduces a special feature to spousal homicide. From information on court proceedings in the Northern Ireland cases, in a small number of cases in which firearms were used, the victims had been married to members of the security forces.

Of the 29 homicides occurring between 1990-1994, 21 were women and eight were men. We also know that there were at least two murder-suicide cases during this time period.[7] What this points to is the need to generate a data set that enumerates the numbers of partners killed, the number of multiple victims, and the number of offenders who committed suicide at the time of the incident. Similarly, the domestic violence homicide data which is presented here refers only to persons known to each other through an intimate sexual relationship. It does not include family members killed at the same time as the domestic violence incident. The deaths of these family members are, however, included in the total homicide figures which means that any calculation of domestic violence homicides as a proportion of total homicides is most likely to be an under-estimate. Since familicide has been identified in domestic violence cases then specific codes need to be designed for use by coroners and police officers, to enable us to determine the extent to which this

---

6. A brief examination of the cause of death from information provided by the courts has been undertaken in Northern Ireland. Similarly files have been accessed in the Belfast Coroner's Court for cases where the husband has killed his wife and subsequently committed suicide. In the majority of familicide cases, reported by the media, the cause of death was shooting.

7. Information collated through a preliminary enquiry at the Belfast Coroner's Court.

phenomenon occurs within the context of domestic violence.[8] Given that most of these deaths have been excluded from the above table, we can say with some confidence that at least 23 per cent of all homicides in Northern Ireland between 1990-1994 (29) were domestic violence related. In other words this percentage would be even higher if the killings of other family members in spousal homicide incidents were to be included.

From the data here (Table 3.2 to 3.5), we can see that between 1990-1994, approximately three women have been killed by their partners for each man killed by his wife or cohabitee (21 female victims, eight male victims). Wilson and Daly (1992) have calculated a spousal sex ratio of killing for England and Wales between 1977-1986.[9] They found that for every 100 men who kill their wives, about 23 women kill their husbands. (We comment later on the importance of contextualising the circumstances in which men and women kill their partners.) As statisticians continue to disaggregate homicide data, it should be possible to calculate the spousal sex ratio of killing for Northern Ireland and make comparisons with other regions of the United Kingdom.

Women as Victims in Spousal Homicide

In 1992 there were six women killed by their male partners in Northern Ireland. In the same year, 120 women were killed by their husbands, common-law husbands or co-habitees in England and Wales (Crime Statistics 1992). Proportionate to the size of population, the Northern Ireland figure for domestic violence related homicides appears relatively high. As Table 3.2 shows, between 1990-1994, 21 women were victims of domestic violence related

---

8. One of the male deaths, recorded in Table 1 above, was in fact a suicide in which the man shot himself following the murder of his wife (uxoricide). This was counted as part of the total homicide figure for that year. From some preliminary work in the Belfast Coroner's Court, we also know that there are at least two other such cases in Northern Ireland as well as a number of cases in which parents, children and in-laws have been killed (familicide). However, further research is needed to determine the exact number of these cases. The point which is being made here is that as a consequence of this the proportion of domestic violence related homicides as recorded above for Northern Ireland, and indeed for other regions of the United Kingdom, under-estimates the real extent of the problem since it relates only to those deaths in which a partner has been killed.

9. The Spousal Sex Ratio Of Killing, SROK, is the number of homicides perpetrated by women per 100 perpetrated by men.

TABLE 3.2
Domestic Violence related Homicides – Northern Ireland,
Republic of Ireland, West Yorkshire, Devon and Cornwall:
Murder, Female Victims

Year	Northern Ireland	Republic of Ireland	West Yorkshire	Devon & Cornwall
1990	Nil	Nil	10	4
1991	6	1	3	4
1992	6	Nil	4	5
1993	4	Nil	10	2
1994	4	Nil	4	3

TABLE 3.3
Domestic Violence related Homicides – Northern Ireland,
Republic of Ireland, West Yorkshire, Devon and Cornwall:
Manslaughter, Female Victims

Year	Northern Ireland	Republic of Ireland	West Yorkshire	Devon & Cornwall
1990	Nil	1	Nil	Nil
1991	Nil	1	Nil	3
1992	1	1	Nil	Nil
1993	Nil	1	Nil	1
1994	Nil	Nil	Nil	Nil

homicide in Northern Ireland. The smaller number of female victims each year in the Republic of Ireland stands in sharp contrast to the Northern Ireland figure, particularly when one considers the difference in population size between the two countries. West Yorkshire has more female victims in 1990 and 1993 than the other areas.[10] In Northern Ireland there were seven female homicides in 1992, which was higher than the other areas.

---

10. An analysis of the ethnic background of the West Yorkshire homicide cases shows that the individuals involved are predominantly of white, European origin.

In Northern Ireland 48 per cent of all female homicides (21 women out of 44) during this five year period were committed by a current or former partner (RUC Crime Statistics 1995). In contrast only 8 per cent of male homicides (7 out of 83) were domestic violence related. Similarly in West Yorkshire, between 1990-1994, 45 per cent of all female homicides related to women killed in interpersonal relationships (West Yorkshire Police Statistics 1995). In Britain 40 per cent of all female homicides are committed by husbands (Crime Statistics 1993). Recent research in the United States suggests that 30 per cent of all women killed each year are slain by their partners (cited in Fineman and Mykitiuk 1994 p.41) and in Canada, domestic violence accounts for 38 per cent of all female homicide victims (Wilson and Daly 1994). It would appear that domestic violence in Britain and Northern Ireland accounts for a larger proportion of the total annual female homicides than in North America. This is due to the smaller proportion of women who are killed by strangers in the United Kingdom relative to the number who are slain in the context of interpersonal relationships. In various countries then, between one-third and one-half of all female killings are domestic violence related.

In all but one of the Northern Ireland female domestic violence killings, the offender was charged with murder. The data in Tables 3.2 and 3.3 refer to the charges recorded by police officers at the time of the incident. This is not necessarily the same charge as that presented at the court hearing. The data for the Republic of Ireland take into account the charge agreed by the Department of Public Prosecutions for court proceedings and which is subsequently recorded in Gardai homicide statistics. This may explain why more offenders of female domestic violence homicide are charged with manslaughter than is the case in Northern Ireland.[11] Such differences in methods of recording make the comparability issue a difficult one to resolve. Similarly, the way in which murder-suicide cases are recorded by various police forces can also make it difficult to compare homicide figures between the different areas. For example, where the offender has committed suicide, and where there has been no trial, then it is difficult to decide in such cases whether the female homicide has been recorded as a manslaughter or a murder.

---

11. On the initial crime report, the Gardai record all domestic violence homicides as murders. When the Department of Public Prosecutions arrive at a decision, the charge may be changed from Murder to manslaughter and it is this which is recorded on the homicide report.

In the collection of the data for this study, much discussion took place around the complication of trying to include those homicides which were not followed by court proceedings, as, for example, in cases where the male offender committed suicide.

Spousal homicide risk and estrangement

Wilson, Daly and Wright (1993) note that an important feature of female domestic violence homicides is the fact that the victim has left the relationship when the incident took place. This points to the need not just to record accurately the current marital status of the victim but also the residency status of the victim and whether the relationship has been terminated. Wilson and Daly (1994) note that in Canada 26 per cent of women killed by their husbands were separated or divorced at the time of the incident.[12] Similarly, Wallace (1986) reported that 98 of 217 women killed by their husbands (as many as 45 per cent) in New South Wales had left their husbands or were in the process of leaving. It seems that the threat of leaving or the fact that the relationship is over is, by itself, sometimes sufficient to create an escalation in the level of violence. Spousal homicide data for New South Wales and Australia also suggest that wives are at risk particularly within the first two months after separation (Wallace 1980; Daly and Wilson 1994).

Since the rate of husbands killing wives is elevated in the aftermath of separation, then leaving a violent relationship can be a very dangerous time for women. This is also a time in which personal safety must be of great concern to those to whom the woman turns for help. One of the problems in providing help for women considering leaving relationships as a result of domestic violence is that although they are aware of the danger they are in, they often do not want to involve friends or relatives since they fear that these too may be pursued by their partner. Support services provided by Women's Aid and the police become crucial at these times. Women who report having their lives threatened in this way need to be treated seriously and provided with urgent attention. Where fatalities can be prevented, then the onus is on help-providers to put in place the appropriate training and resources to do so.

---

12. Using Canadian homicide data for 1974-1992, researchers have shown that whilst 3.8 wives were killed per slain husband in co-residing couples, this ratio increased to 10.1 wives per slain husband amongst separated couples (Wilson and Daly 1994).

Men as Victims in Spousal Homicide

TABLE 3.4
Domestic Violence related Homicides – Northern Ireland,
Republic of Ireland, West Yorkshire, Devon and Cornwall:
Murder, Male Victims

Year	Northern Ireland	Republic of Ireland	West Yorkshire	Devon & Cornwall
1990	Nil	Nil	1	NIl
1991	2	Nil	1	1
1992	2	2	1	Nil
1993	3	1	1	2
1994	Nil	Nil	Nil	1

TABLE 3.5
Domestic Violence related Homicides – Northern Ireland,
Republic of Ireland, West Yorkshire, Devon and Cornwall:
Manslaughter, Male Victims

Year	Northern Ireland	Republic of Ireland	West Yorkshire	Devon & Cornwall
1990	Nil	Nil	Nil	Nil
1991	Nil	Nil	Nil	Nil
1992	Nil	1	Nil	Nil
1993	Nil	Nil	Nil	Nil
1994	Nil	1	Nil	Nil

The overall number of women killing their partners is small. Table 3.4 however shows that more women have killed their partners in Northern Ireland than in any of the regional comparators. Given the current controversy surrounding such killings, it is worth investigating the extent to which a previous history of domestic violence provided the grounds for diminished responsibility, provocation or self-defence. We shall see later that there is some evidence from court proceedings

(Tables 3.11 and 3.13) that the history of violence against the female defendant is taken into account. In two of the cases, the charge was reduced to manslaughter on grounds of provocation. The most important point to note here is that in six out of the seven trials, a previous history of domestic violence against the woman was noted. It has been estimated that up to three-quarters of women convicted of killing their partners, will have been battered often over a prolonged period of time (Horder 1992). However in cases in which men kill their partners, battering is rarely cited as a defence or a precipitating factor. There are clearly gender differences in the reasons cited for domestic violence homicides.

It appears that the cause of death also differs between the sexes. Whilst men were more likely to use firearms, beatings and strangulations, more women stabbed their husbands (see Tables 3.10 to 3.13). These sex differences in the relative uses of different weapons in spousal homicide are paralleled in the United States and Britain (Wilson and Daly 1993). Interestingly, the police report forms on incidents of domestic violence now record whether the individual has had access to a firearm. These reports are used to collate statistical information for the RUC and will enable an analysis to be undertaken in the future on the extent to which firearms are used in situations of domestic violence.

Attempted Murder

TABLE 3.6
Domestic Violence related Attempted Murder – Northern Ireland,
Republic of Ireland, West Yorkshire, Devon and Cornwall:
Female Victims

Year	Northern Ireland	Republic of Ireland	West Yorkshire	Devon & Cornwall
1990	Not available	Nil	1	Not available
1991	Not available	Nil	6	Not available
1992	4	Nil	7	Not available
1993	8	Nil	2	Not available
1994	5	Nil	3	2

TABLE 3.7
Domestic Violence related Attempted Murder – Northern Ireland,
Republic of Ireland, West Yorkshire, Devon and Cornwall:
Male Victims

Year	Northern Ireland	Republic of Ireland	West Yorkshire	Devon & Cornwall
1990	Not available	Nil	Nil	Not available
1991	Not available	Nil	Nil	Not available
1992	1	Nil	2	Not available
1993	2	Nil	Nil	Not available
1994	2	Nil	3	Nil

Men are much more likely to attempt murder than their female partners. In Northern Ireland the ratio is 3:1 (Tables 3.6 and 3.7). The explanations offered by assailants, and by women who have survived attempts on their lives, suggest that the killer was motivated by sexual jealousy and/or by the woman's attempt to terminate the relationship (Mahoney 1994). Declarations like 'if I can't have her, nobody else can' are recurring features of such cases and the perpetrators of attempted murder frequently threaten to kill themselves also (McWilliams and McKiernan 1993). The trial comments reported later in this chapter (Table 3.11), also reveal a history of sub-lethal violence. This is an important point, since homicidal husbands often engage in a pattern of previous violence including attempted murder. These threats to kill need to be taken seriously by prosecutors and should be interpreted not only as coercive tactics that serve to terrorize abused women and to keep them under control but also as potential precursors to murder. Even after men have served prison sentences for previous acts of violence, they often continue to threaten their partners. In one of the cases, reported in Table 3.11, six months after his release from prison, the husband made a repeated attempt to murder his wife, finally succeeding in killing both her mother and sister.

McWilliams and McKiernan (1993) report that a frequent threat from husbands, whose violence was escalated by the wife's departure, was 'I swear if you ever leave me, I'll find you and kill you.' As Daly and Wilson (1993) note 'although violent coercion and threats

may serve the proprietary husband's interests by intimidating his victim, they also raise her incentives to escape the relationship, which may in turn lead to escalated coercion.' The fact that women who leave proprietary husbands may be pursued and murdered is known to police, to refuge workers, and to others who have direct experience of domestic violence, but it still does not appear to be taken sufficiently seriously by those responsible for prosecuting these offences.

Women who stay with abusive husbands because they are afraid to leave may be aware that their departure would elevate or spread the risk of lethal assault. Fear of potentially lethal violence must also be added to the economic and other reasons why abused women do not leave the relationship, particularly when it seems to those unfamiliar with the circumstances that it is the obvious thing to do (McWilliams and McKiernan 1993). Fear of repeated attacks is also what drives many women to seek anonymity on leaving violent relationships. In some cases, women who have had their lives threatened are too frightened to take out exclusion orders since their whereabouts is made known to their abusers.[13] Similarly the usual legal construction of 'imminent danger' as immediate and the six month restriction on exclusion orders are both inadequate in cases where abusive husbands continue to stalk their partners.

There needs to be more quantitative assessment of the magnitude of heightened homicide risk and sub-lethal violence incurred by women who have separated from their husbands or who have left relationships. With improved data sets, it should be possible to undertake such research throughout the United Kingdom particularly if residency status is recorded in the crime reports.

Serious assault

Approximately 95 per cent of the serious assaults in domestic violence incidents recorded under the Offences Against the Person Act are committed by men. In Northern Ireland between 1992-1994, there were just under one thousand serious assaults on women by their male partners. The majority (58 per cent) of these assaults were carried out by current or former husbands, and two out of every

---

13. Any address from which the person is excluded is written on the court order.

five serious assaults on women involve a common-law husband or boyfriend. Table 3.8 excludes assaults involving rape. RUC crime statistics for 1992 show that there were 19 rapes by men of their female partners (wives or cohabitees) and a further two women were assaulted with intent to rape by their male partners.

The tables presented here deal only with the most serious forms of assault. In a subsequent chapter of this report, we deal with common assault cases presented at five Magistrates courts in Northern Ireland. Common assault is the most frequently recorded crime in relation to domestic violence offences. Currently there is no breakdown of these offences by sex and relationship of victim to offender. As a result, we do not know the extent to which common assaults take place in the context of domestic violence in Northern Ireland. Since this material cannot be presented here, we are unable to make a comparison between the numbers involved, from the least to the most serious forms of assault. It is imperative that such data are recorded since the prevalence of common assault would present a more accurate picture of the extent of domestic violence within the criminal justice system. It is a sobering thought that despite the lesser likelihood of serious assaults relative to common assaults, there are still sufficiently high numbers of serious assaults to make domestic violence an everyday event in the criminal courts in Northern Ireland.

In 1994, for example, there were 360 serious assaults (Table 3.8) and, as we have seen, five attempted murders of women (Table 3.6). *This means that at least one woman in Northern Ireland reported a serious assault by her male partner for every day of the year.*

The most common form of serious assault is Assault Occasioning Actual Bodily Harm (AOABH, Section 47 of Offences Against the Person Act). The types of injuries related to AOABH include minor fractures, cuts requiring stitches, a broken nose, the loss or breaking of teeth or a temporary loss of consciousness resulting from such injuries. In the context of domestic assaults, there were 925 offenders (886 men and 39 women) charged with AOABH between 1992-1994. This figure gives us some indication of the extent of medical attention required when victims present with these injuries.

No other assaults approach these numbers. The next most common charge is that of Grievous Bodily Harm (GBH) or Section 20 of the Offences Against the Person Act. Again it is worth noting the types

TABLE 3.8
Assaults Related to Domestic Violence in Northern Ireland 1992–1994*

	1992			1993			1994		
	Female Victims	Male Victims	Total	Female Victims	Male Victims	Total	Female Victims	Male Victims	Total
GBH, GBH with Intent and Attempted GBH	18	2	20	13	2	15	19	5	25
Wounding with Intent	1	2	3	3	1	4	–	1	1
AOABH	238	7	245	324	12	336	324	20	344
Threats to Kill	9		9	11	–	11	17	–	17
Intimidation	2	–	2	–	–	–	–	–	–
TOTAL	268	11	279	351	15	366	360	26	386

Source: RUC Statistics, July 1995

*   These were the only years for which data was available.

of injuries related to this charge. These include injury resulting in permanent disability, permanent loss of sensory functions, serious disfigurement, broken bones including fractured skull and broken ribs, injuries causing a substantial loss of blood or very serious psychiatric injury. In the context of violent assaults related to domestic violence, it is important to note that the cases which come to police attention under-estimate the extent to which these kinds of incidents occur. Nonetheless, these figures serve as a reminder of the length to which some offenders will go in inflicting harm on their partners.

Wounding with Intent (Section 18 of the Offences Against the Person Act), Threats to Kill and Intimidation carry with them the most severe penalties. As with GBH, however, these charges may sometimes be the outcome of a review process which can involve a reduction from a more serious charge particularly where police officers make a judgement that the evidential proof is not sufficient to sustain the initial charge. Moreover, the charge recorded by the police can be further reviewed by the Department of Public Prosecutions.

The extent to which such reviews involve reduced charges is not known but indications from court proceedings (Table 3.10) point to this. For example, one offender who was charged by the RUC with Attempted Murder (Table 3.13) was instead prosecuted for 'Wounding With Intent'. The decision to prosecute and the choice of charge is determined by the availability of sufficient evidence to establish a particular intent.

Prosecuting domestic violence in Northern Ireland

Clearly, the decisions to review charges requires some further discussion. When such reviews involve a reduction of charges by court prosecutors this can affect victim confidence and requires much more attention than it has received to date. Part of the function of the DPP is to ensure that cases which are likely to result in judge-directed or other acquittals are not proceeded with, and to check that charges are laid at the right level of seriousness. The police may make an initial decision under which charge to proceed; but they do so knowing that the DPP may possibly alter the charge. Prosecutions are only initiated or continued by the DPP where the Director is satisfied that: 1) the evidence which can be adduced in court is sufficient to provide a reasonable prospect of obtaining a conviction; and 2) prosecution is required in the public interest. Alterna-

tively, the DPP may decide that the case should not be proceeded with, either because of lack of evidence or because to proceed would not be in the public interest.

Those responsible for making decisions on prosecution need to be aware of the special difficulties which arise in dealing with offences of domestic violence. When prosecutors reduce charges which, in turn, results in lighter sentences these decisions need to be clearly explained to the victim or to the deceased victim's family. The DPP argue that the directions to prosecute are issued after careful consideration of the evidence and the choice of charge is determined based on the facts of the case. They also state that in some instances a further assessment of the prosecution case or the defence case, at or near trial, may suggest that the prosecution of a defendant is no longer warranted on the charge, or charges, originally directed but is warranted in some further or other charge, or charges. The DPP also note that there is a duty on the prosecuting authority to keep the decision to prosecute, and the appropriateness of the charges, under constant review. They point out that circumstances, such as the provision of medical or psychological evidence by the defence often shortly before trial, can arise which warrant the prosecution accepting a plea to a charge of manslaughter on the basis that, if the matter proceeded to trial, there no longer remained a reasonable prospect of obtaining a conviction for murder. The DPP emphasise that in determining whether it is appropriate to accept a plea to a lesser charge, or to accept a plea of guilty to one charge while not proceeding with another, a pre-eminent consideration is to ensure that the court is not left in the position of being unable to pass an appropriate sentence consistent with the gravity of the conduct of the defendant which the prosecution can prove.[14]

The decision to review the initial charge, or the acceptance of a lesser charge at or near a trial (commonly known as downgrading) can cause considerable dismay to victims or their families, particularly when they have not received any rationale for this. Given the lack of familiarity with the prosecution system, individuals who have been subjected to abusive assaults deserve to be kept informed about their case and given reasons as to why the initial charge has been reduced. If victim confidence is to be enhanced in the criminal justice system

---

14. This information was provided by the DPP (N.Ireland) and is outlined in the CPS Prosecution Guidelines on Domestic Violence.

then procedures need to be introduced which enable prosecutors to explain the various steps being taken to ensure a successful prosecution. If victims, who are often the survivors of repetitive, serious and life threatening incidents, are not included throughout the preliminary enquiry and at the final stages then the outcome can leave them not only with a sense of disillusionment but also with a sense that a terrible miscarriage of justice has occurred. In Canada, Australia and the United States, a prosecutor mandated victim support service has been introduced in relation to domestic violence in order to facilitate this process. Clearly some thought needs to be given to initiating such a service in this country. This could take the form of either a well resourced independent victim witness support service for domestic violence cases or as part of a co-ordinated prosecution system's response to domestic violence.

The cases reported in Tables 3.9-3.13 refer to court proceedings which took place between 1989-1994. This information, including the comments in the final column of Tables 3.10-3.13, has been provided by the Department of Public Prosecutions. Some of these cases directly relate to the incidents recorded by the police (and outlined in the previous tables), but we do not know the extent of this overlap since the information provided by the RUC was anonymised. An attempt was made to cross-check the data sets and

TABLE 3.9
Prosecutions for Murder, Attempted Murder and Manslaughter related to Domestic Violence, Northern Ireland, 1989–1994

Verdict	Female Victims			Male Victims	
	Murder	Attempted	Manslaughter	Murder	Manslaughter
Convicted as charged	4	1	1	–	1
Convicted of lesser charge	6	7		5	
Acquitted/ Not Guilty	–	1		2	1
TOTAL	10	9	1	7	2

Source: Department of Public Prosecutions

it was apparent that there were cases charged by the police which had not yet reached the prosecution stage.

Given the time constraints of this study, we were unable to compare the outcomes of these court proceedings with those of non-domestic violence cases. As we show later, in the chapter on Magistrates Courts, this is a useful exercise as it gives us some idea of the equity in sentencing between cases which involve those in intimate relationships and those which do not. This is an area which requires much more research. Given the lack of information which currently exists, we draw on the findings of a study recently undertaken for a series of Channel 4 programmes on violence in Britain (Culf 1995). The researchers involved monitored all crown court cases in England and Wales between June and September, 1995 and found that:

- one-third of 85 murder cases was classified as being related to domestic violence; 24 involved men killing female partners and four involved women who had killed their male partners;

- compared to 46 per cent of the domestic killings in which either a plea of guilty to manslaughter was accepted, or the jury returned a manslaughter verdict, only 32 per cent non-domestic violence killings resulted in manslaughter convictions;

- of all domestic violence killings, only 39 per cent ended in a conviction for murder compared to 53 per cent of non-domestic violence cases;

- prison sentences in domestic violence manslaughters are substantially lower than for non-domestic violence cases with most men convicted of manslaughter receiving a sentence of four years or less;

- diminished responsibility was the favoured ground for defence in cases in which the defendant pleaded guilty to manslaughter, rather than provocation or no intent.

With these findings in mind we now turn to the cases presented by the DPP in Northern Ireland.

Verdict and Sentencing: Men who kill

In six out of the ten cases (Table 3.10) in which the male defendant was charged with murder of his female partner, a verdict of man-

TABLE 3.10
Domestic Violence related Prosecutions – Northern Ireland, 1989–1994: Murder, Female Victims

Case and Age Victim	Case and Age Defendant	Relationship	Verdict and Sentence	Comments
Q, 22 years	Q, 21 years	Husband and Wife	Manslaughter (acquitted of murder). 3 years imprisonment.	Strangulation. Provocation – persistent abuse, including stabbing defendant in leg.
G, 38 years	G, 43 years	Husband and Wife	Manslaughter (medical evidence regarding capacity to form intent). 3 years imprisonment, suspended 2 years.	Drink problem. Personal Protection/Exclusion Orders. Found wife with another man.
B, 33 years	B, 36 years	Boyfriend/Girlfriend	Murder but insane. Hospital order.	
B, 29 years	M, 21 years	Boyfriend/Girlfriend	Murder. Life imprisonment.	Shot dead girlfriend and two males.
W, 27 years	W, 30 years	Husband and Wife	Murder. Life imprisonment.	Shot dead wife with legally-held gun.
Q, 26 years	O, 34 years	Husband and Wife	Manslaughter (diminished responsibility). 5 years imprisonment.	
T, 32 years	L, 35 years	Co-habitees	Manslaughter (difficulties in proving intent and causation). 5 years imprisonment.	Previous violence towards deceased. Victim died of injuries suffered in drunken row.
T, 20 years	C, 29 years	Co-habitees	Manslaughter – guilty plea: provocation. 6 years imprisonment.	Strangulation. Provocation based on infidelity.
O, 46 years	D, 46 years	Ex-co-habitees	Manslaughter. 4 years imprisonment.	No evidence of intent to kill. Conflicting medical evidence as to cause of death. Previous domestic violence by defendant towards deceased.
M, 40 years	M, 38 years	Former girlfriend/ boyfriend	Murder. Life imprisonment.	Previous history of violence towards deceased.

* Further investigation is required to ascertain the detailed background to each case and any conclusions must be considered with a degree of circumspection.

slaughter was returned on the grounds of diminished responsibility or provocation. The way in which provocation has been interpreted in some of these cases has led to concern amongst those working in the field of domestic violence. For example, Women's Aid have publicly stated their concern following cases in which provocation, such as 'persistent nagging' or 'sexual taunts' are seen as constituting part of the abuse to which defendants were subjected and which, in turn, allowed their violent responses to be mitigated.

In other court proceedings, extra-marital relationships have been understood to constitute provocation and appear to have worked to the advantage of men who have killed their wives. Manslaughter verdicts have thus been allowed on the grounds that extra-marital behaviour has caused men to kill in a moment of 'sudden loss of self-control'. Excessive use of alcohol has also been seen as part of the mitigating circumstances in domestic violence homicides, despite evidence pointing to a previous history of persistent violence. Concern is voiced by agencies supporting the families of victims when such evidence is accepted in mitigation despite the previous offending behaviour.

Verdict and Sentencing: Women who Kill

Similarly, the question of justice for women who have killed their husbands or partners after experiencing years of violent abuse has also been brought to recent public attention. Campaigns on behalf of women (Southall Black sisters and Justice for Women) who have killed violent husbands have arisen out of contested legal definitions of provocation, diminished responsibility and self-defence. One group has proposed a new defence of 'self-preservation' which would take into account the contextual, and gendered, nature of domestic violence (Radford and Kelly, 1995). Hague and Mallos (1993) note that the Home Affairs Committee on domestic violence rejected the introduction of this new defence of self-preservation which would differ from self-defence because it would not require an immediately preceding life-threatening incident. The committee also rejected changes to the current definition of 'sufficient force' in self-defence to allow for women's lesser physical strength. Recent appeal decisions have given rise to increased discussion about the precarious mental state which can result from persistent abuse.

TABLE 3.11
Domestic Violence related Prosecutions – Northern Ireland, 1989–1994: Murder, Male Victims

Case and Age Victim	Case and Age Defendant	Relationship	Verdict and Sentence	Comments
G, 33 years	G, 38 years	Husband and Wife	Manslaughter (diminished responsibility). 2 years imprisonment, suspended 2 years.	Stabbed with kitchen knife. History of domestic violence and depression.
O, 47 years	O, 46 years	Husband and Wife	Manslaughter. 2 years imprisonment, suspended 12 months.	Stabbed with kitchen knife. Previous violence by deceased husband.
B, 35 years	B, 31 years	Husband and Wife	Manslaughter (provocation). Probation 3 years.	Stabbed during row. Previous domestic violence. Deceased husband had convictions for assault and disorderly behaviour.
S, 41 years	S, 41 years	Husband and Wife	Acquitted.	Wife shot dead husband with legally held gun but acquitted. Previous domestic violence by husband.
T, 38 years	T, 41 years	Husband and Wife	Manslaughter (provocation). 3 years imprisonment, suspended 3 years.	
A, 29 years	M, 28 years	Co-habitees	Manslaughter. 4 years imprisonment, suspended 4 years.	Stabbed in course of argument. Previous history of domestic violence by deceased towards defendant.
E, 38 years	E, 36 years	Husband and Wife	Acquitted.	Admitted to stabbing deserting husband but acquitted.

* Further investigation is required to ascertain the detailed background to each case and any conclusions must be considered with a degree of circumspection.

TABLE 3.12

Domestic Violence related Prosecutions – Northern Ireland, 1989–1994: Manslaughter

Female Victims

Case and Age Victim	Case and Age Defendant	Relationship	Verdict and Sentence	Comments
L, 37 years	B, 38 years	Co-habitees	Guilty plea. 3 years imprisonment.	Deceased was dropped out of upper storey window. Previous domestic violence by defendant towards deceased.

Male Victims

Case and Age Victim	Case and Age Defendant	Relationship	Verdict and Sentence	Comments
B, 45 years	B, 43 years	Husband and Wife	Guilty plea. Probation for 3 years.	Stabbed with kitchen knife during argument.
R, 38 years	R, 35 years	Husband and wife	Not guilty.	Self-defence. Previous history of domestic violence.

* Further investigation is required to ascertain the detailed background to each case and any conclusions must be considered with a degree of circumspection.

The increased recognition that long-term abuse can cause a 'slow build-up' of anger leading to a violent response, has offered the possibility that women who have killed their partners may be considered in a more sympathetic light. In Australia in the 1950s a partial defence known as 'excessive defence' was allowed in cases where the person taking action acts beyond the necessity of the occasion and kills the offender. It was abolished some years later although it is now being recommended by some lawyers as a defence for battered women who kill (Horder 1995).

Six out of seven murder cases reported in Table 3.11, in which women have been charged with the murder of their male partners, show evidence of a previous history of domestic violence. In these six cases, this evidence, which was allowed to be heard, led to verdicts of manslaughter and, in one case, to an acquittal. The fact that none of these women received an immediate prison sentence makes the situation in Northern Ireland appear somewhat different from the rest of the United Kingdom. Elsewhere, there have been on-going public campaigns to have women in similar situations released from prison. What is clearly needed is some central system of recording prosecutions related to domestic violence. The recommendation of the Home Affairs Committee that the Crown Prosecution Service should gather regional and national figures on prosecution, and remedy existing regional disparities, is very important in trying to ensure that there is some consistency in prosecution policy throughout the country. This recommendation should also apply to Northern Ireland.

Verdict and Sentencing: Attempted murder

Table 3.13 refers to cases in which nine men were prosecuted for attempting to kill their partners. In only one out of the nine cases was a verdict of guilty to the charge of attempted murder returned. Of the eight defendants who either pleaded guilty or were found guilty of these assaults, only two received immediate prison sentences. Although imprisonment may not always be desirable, it is very important that serious offences are not seen to be trivialized or treated differently to other offences of similar gravity. Organisations and professionals working with abused women report their frustration at the sentencing policy in such cases (McWilliams and McKiernan, 1993). After the trauma involved for a woman in going

TABLE 3.13
Domestic Violence related Prosecutions – Northern Ireland, 1989–1994: Attempted Murder, Female Victims

Case and Age Victim	Case and Age Defendant	Relationship	Verdict and Sentence	Comments
C, 29 years	C, 45 years	Husband and Wife separated	Wounding with intent. 4 years imprisonment.	Serious assault with knife, chainsaw and strangulation. Previous convictions. Following release from prison, defendant murdered sister-in-law, and mother-in-law and attempted murder of wife.
C	M, 30 years	Ex-Boyfriend/ Grilfriend	GBH with intent. 4 years imprisonment, suspended 3 years.	Previous domestic violence history. Previous convictions.
Q	Q, 46 years	Husband and Wife	GBH with intent. 30 months imprisonment, suspended 18 months.	History of violence.
M, 37 years	M, 51 years	Common Law Husband and Wife	GBH with intent (mental illness). Probation 3 years.	One previous assault on victim. Breach of Order relating to wife (not victim).
D, 25 years	P, 25 years	Former Boyfriend/ Girlfriend	Acquitted.	
M, 44 years	M, 48 years	Husband and Wife	Attempted murder. Probation 3 years.	Tried to poison wife and two sons after marriage breakdown. Previous domestic violence by accused. Personal Protection/Exclusion Orders in force.
V	S, 22 years	Co-habitees (engaged to be married)	Malicious wounding. 2 years imprisonment, suspended 3 years.	Shot victim with legally held gun during argument. Previous history of domestic violence by accused towards injured party.
M	M, 48 years	Husband and Wife	Attempted wounding with intent to cause GBH. 5 years imprisonment, suspended 3 years.	Previous history of domestic violence by accused towards injured party.
W	W, 46 years	Husband and Wife separated	Wounding with intent to cause GBH. 6 years imprisonment.	Previous history of domestic violence by accused towards injured party. Previous conviction.

through the prosecution process, the provision of a suspended sentence or probation, alongside the kinds of remarks which can be made during the court proceedings about the nature of their relationship, can give offenders the impression that attacks on their partners are being condoned by the justice system.

Conclusion

The findings in this chapter point to the extent and seriousness of domestic violence. Between 1990-1994, 23 per cent of all homicides were accounted for by the murder or manslaughter of a marital or cohabiting partner. Of the total number of female homicides, 48 per cent took place in the context of domestic violence. There were many more domestic violence homicides in Northern Ireland (29) compared to the Republic of Ireland (10) between 1990-1994. The spousal homicide rate (1.9) is higher in Northern Ireland than in countries such as Canada, and the proportion of non-security homicides which are domestic violence related appears to be higher in Northern Ireland than in other comparable regions. We can only speculate about the reasons for this.

The focus of police resources, until relatively recently, on political violence in contrast to domestic violence may be one explanation. The more limited opportunities for women to leave the violent relationship, the more traditional attitudes towards the insolubility of marriage, the more conservative views towards women's role in the family and the increase in tolerance towards forms of violence which might in other situations be regarded as 'unacceptable' may all be factors which might help to explain the higher number of fatalities in the context of domestic violence in Northern Ireland. Until further research is undertaken on the causation of death, we do not know the extent to which the availability of firearms in people's own homes played a role in domestic violence homicides. Certainly, combined with some of the factors noted above it may be an additional factor in the Northern Ireland situation.

The chapter also notes the number of domestic violence related serious assaults (such as AOABH and GBH) and attempted murders which took place in recent years in Northern Ireland. Decisions to review charges in relation to these crimes and the subsequent prosecution outcomes have been noted here. It is apparent that where there is a persistent history of violence against the female

partner, it does need to be taken into account. If the incident is taken out of context, and treated as a one-off, then the victim will perceive that the assault on her is not being taken sufficiently seriously. It is taken into account by the prosecuting authority in deciding, for example, if the injury was accidental or if it is in the public interest to prosecute. Similarly, if the defendant is found guilty, past convictions are taken into account in sentencing. Where the difficulty lies is the extent to which past behaviour can be considered admissible in the actual trial proceedings. The exception to the rule on past behaviour or convictions is the rule on similar fact evidence (see Murphy 1995). Past events are relevant if they are so strikingly similar to the offence charged as to identify the offence as the hallmark of the accused, or undermine a defence such as accident. But this type of evidence is very difficult to distinguish from mere evidence of disposition that the crime conforms to the defendant's character, which is not admissible. In any event, the judge has a discretion to exclude evidence, the prejudicial nature of which outweighs its probative value. This strikes at the very heart of domestic violence cases, where the murder is usually the last event in a long chain; none of the previous events being so strikingly similar as to be admissible, but all being necessary to a full understanding of the situation.

Despite the serious nature and high level of domestic violence cases prosecuted at the Crown Court, it is important to note that by far the largest proportion of Offences Against The Person cases are heard in Magistrates Courts. It is to this particular part of the judicial system that we now turn.

FOUR

Prosecutions and Sentencing of Domestic Violence Offences in Five Northern Ireland Magistrates Courts

In this chapter, we review the results of research conducted in five Magistrates Courts in Northern Ireland, in order to provide a small-scale study of the incidence of domestic violence cases in these courts and of the range of sentencing for this type of offence. There has been surprisingly little research of this kind undertaken in the UK. Smith (1989) in her chapter on the prosecution process discusses in detail the work of only two researchers (Wasoff 1982; Sanders 1987) who have studied the prosecution and sentencing of domestic violence offences in British courts. A recent study of the response to domestic violence in Hull (Kewley and Cromack 1994) presents global figures for the offences of assault (AOABH), wounding and common assault dealt with at Magistrates Courts throughout Humberside from 1990-1993, but the researchers state that it is not possible to indicate what degree of domestic violence cases are subsumed under these headings, because such cases are not separately recorded or documented. This point regarding a lack of separate recording of domestic violence cases applies also to the Northern Ireland Court Service.

The present study aims to shed some light on the question of what proportion of violent offences before Magistrates Courts are actually domestic violence related and how these cases are treated by the courts. We start by outlining the methods we used to obtain our data, then we turn to the results which deal, first, with the prosecutions and, second, the sentencing for offences related to domestic violence at these five courts. In respect of one offence, Assault Occasioning Actual Bodily Harm, Section 47 (AOABH), a comparison of sentencing will be made between cases where the offence involved male to male violence and cases where it was committed in a domestic context by a man against a woman. In addition, we make some comparisons between the prosecution outcomes in domestic violence cases and outcomes for Violence Against the Person offences for all courts in Northern Ireland in 1994. Brief case studies extracted from

police files of four domestic violence cases before these courts are included, to indicate the nature of the violence involved.

Methods

With the permission of the Northern Ireland Court Service, five Magistrates Courts were visited to examine daily court order books recording criminal offences for a six month period, January to June 1994. The courts, Bangor, Coleraine, Downpatrick, Lisburn and Newtownabbey, were chosen partly to provide a geographical spread in the North and East of the province but also because another part of this research, on breaches of civil protection orders (see Chapter 5) was being conducted at these courts. It is important to note that the study was not intended to be a representative one but rather a useful insight into how domestic violence is dealt with at each of these courts.

At each court, details of all *Offences against the Person* recorded in the daily court order books for the specified period were noted, ie. offences ranging from common assault (Section 42) through the more serious charges up to and including murder. From this information, it was possible to establish a breakdown of these offences according to gender: male to male; female to female; male to female; and female to male violence. Cases of *criminal damage* were also extracted, but in this instance, only those cases which involved male and female defendants/victims were noted. These cases include damage to property, such as broken windows and forced entry, and are typical of the type of criminal damage involved in the context of a domestic violence incident.

Breach of the Peace charges

Grace (1995) in her Home Office study states that police officers in England and Wales frequently prosecute domestic violence cases as Breach of the Peace, perhaps because the charge does not require the complainant's evidence. Because of the number of these charges and the daunting nature of the task involved in verifying each one, it was decided that it had to be outside the scope of the present research to include this category of offence, but it is certainly possible that a number of domestic violence cases in Northern Ireland lie hidden under this charge and this should be borne in mind in interpreting the results.

The next step was to determine what proportion of male/female and female/male offences against the person and criminal damage offences was domestic violence related. Magistrate's Courts' records generally provide scant information, with only brief details of the defendant and victim and the nature of the crime. In some cases, there was enough information to establish that it was indeed a domestic violence offence, i.e. the case was a breach of a personal protection or exclusion order or a note on the record stated 'ex-wife' or 'wife gave evidence'. In other cases, it was clearly not a domestic violence case, e.g. an attack on a police officer of the opposite sex or a female traffic warden or store detective. The fact that two parties shared the same surname suggested the likelihood that they were, or had been, husband and wife but no firm assumptions were made, except in the few cases where a note on the court record confirmed the supposition. In order to distinguish the domestic violence cases, within our terms of reference, from stranger violence or disputes between acquaintances or other family members, it was necessary, in the majority of cases, to seek verification by other means. This was done by one of two methods:

1. It was sometimes possible to verify a case by consulting the records of civil personal protection and exclusion orders in the same court. The existence of such an order, naming the same parties as featured in the criminal record, within a twelve-month period of the date of the offence, was taken to be sound evidence that the case in question was a domestic one. Twenty-one cases were verified by this means.

2   Since not all victims of assault are or have been in possession of a civil order, in the majority of cases it was necessary to seek verification from the police. A note was taken from the court record of the RUC station where the offence was charged and RUC Process Offices were then contacted with details and asked to state, after reference to case files, whether or not the case was domestic violence related. (A definition of 'domestic violence' was supplied.) All of the RUC Process Offices replied but in some cases, verification was not possible because case files were unavailable. This applied to nine cases (11 per cent) of the 81 submitted to the RUC for verification.

In total, verification was sought, by one of the above described methods, for 153 cases (137 male and female defendants on Offences Against the Person charges and 18 male and female defendants on criminal damage only charges). For those needing verification, 49 per cent of the defendants (67) on Offences Against the Person charges, and 55 per cent of defendants (10) on criminal damage only charges were confirmed as domestic violence offenders.

Prosecutions

A breakdown of the results of research in the five magistrates' courts is provided in table form (Table 4.1). The tables indicate the total number of defendants tried on Offences Against the Person charges in each court in the six-month survey period and analyse the percentages of male to male, female to female, female to male and male to female violence.[1]

The boxes on the left hand side of Table 4.1 show all the Offences Against the Person as recorded in the five courts. Taking these offences as a whole, before we take the specific cases of domestic violence, the figures break down as follows:

- On average 61 per cent of the cases before the courts is male to male violence.

- The average figure for female-female assaults is 8 per cent.

- Female to male violence averages at only 4 per cent, most of this being assaults on the police.

- Male to female violence varies from 19 per cent – 26 per cent of cases before the courts, with an average figure of 23 per cent across the five courts.

There are two points to note here. The first is that most violent offences prosecuted in the courts involve violence between adult males.[2] The second point, and the most important one for the

---

1 Criminal damage only charges are not included in this table. They are included in the tables on sentencing.

2 Many of these prosecutions include assaults on the police (involving almost 50 per cent of the cases at Lisburn).

TABLE 4.1
Offences against the Person, January–June 1994 (5 Courts)

Bangor

Total No. of Defendants	M/M		M/M & F		F/F		F/M		M/F		Domestic Violence Sub-Set		
	No.	%	No.	%	No.	%	No.	%	No.	%	Male Defendants	Female Defendants	DV %
80	55*	69	3	4	3	4	2**	3	17	21	10	0	13

* Male–male includes 13 attacks on police   ** Female–male both cases assaults on policemen

Coleraine

Total No. of Defendants	M/M		M/C		M/M&F		F/F		F/M & F		F/M		M/F		Domestic Violence Sub-Set		
	No.	%	No.	%	No.	%	No.	%	No.	%	No.	%	No.	%	Male Defendants	Female Defendants	DV %
133	82*	61	5	4	2	1	11**	8	3	2	1	1	29	22	15	0	11

* Male–male includes 17 attacks on police   ** Female–female includes 1 assault on police

Downpatrick

Total No. of Defendants	M/M		M/C		M/M&F		F/F		F/M		M/F		Domestic Violence Sub-Set		
	No.	%	No.	%	No.	%	No.	%	No.	%	No.	%	Male Defendants	Female Defendants	DV %
95	43	45	3	3	5	5	12	13	7*	7	25*	26	17	0	18

* Female–male includes 5 attacks on policemen   ** Male–female includes 1 assault on policewoman

Lisburn

Total No. of Defendants	M/M		M/M & F		F/F		F/M		M/F		Domestic Violence Sub-Set		
	No.	%	No.	%	No.	%	No.	%	No.	%	Male Defendants	Female Defendants	DV %
67	42*	63	1	1	3	4	2**	3	17	25	14	0	21

* Male–male includes 20 attacks on police   ** Female–male includes 2 attacks on police

Newtownabbey

Total No. of Defendants	M/M		M/M & F		F/F		F/M		M/F		Domestic Violence Sub-Set		
	No.	%	No.	%	No.	%	No.	%	No.	%	Male Defendants	Female Defendants	DV %
99	66*	66	2	2	10	10	2**	2	19	19	11	0	11

* Male–male includes 14 attacks on police   ** Female–male includes 1 attack on police

Key   M/M   – male to male assaults   F/F   – female to female assaults
       M/C   – male assaults on child/young person   F/M   – female to male assaults
       M/M & F – male assaults on a male and female   M/F   – male to female assaults

purposes of this study, is that as many as one in five of all Offences Against the Person coming before these courts is male to female violence.

In Table 4.1 we have also extracted all the domestic violence cases and have presented these in the boxes on the right hand side, the final three columns, of each row. In other words the domestic violence cases become a sub-set of all the Offences Against the Person.

The first thing to note here is that all defendants are male.[3] It is possible that women are not normally prosecuted on domestic violence charges in the five areas studied, but it is more likely, as research elsewhere suggests, that this is overwhelmingly a crime perpetrated by men against women.

The percentage of all Offences Against the Person at each court that are domestic violence related is presented in the final column and varies from 11 per cent to 21 per cent. In total, the number of verified domestic violence defendants at these five courts was 67, representing an average figure of 14 per cent of all offences committed.

Table 4.2 illustrates domestic violence as a percentage of all male-female violence in the five courts and shows that an average 64 per cent of prosecutions for assaults by men on women relate to a domestic context.

TABLE 4.2
Domestic Violence as a Percentage of Male-Female Violence,
January-June 1994 (5 Courts)

Bangor %	Coleraine %	Downpatrick %	Lisburn %	Newtownabbey %	Average %
59	52	68	82	58	64

A number of further points must be emphasized here:

1. It is possible that a distortion of the figures for domestic violence is introduced by the inclusion of Bangor and Coleraine

---

3 Although all the domestic violence defendants in Table 1 are male, two of the defendants on criminal damage alone charges were female.

Magistrates Courts. In these areas, brawls amongst seasonal visitors to the seaside resorts of Bangor and Portrush may account for a disproportionate amount of violence. Similarly, Newtownabbey Magistrates Court's location in the Greater Belfast area may mean that it processes a greater number of sectarian or security-related offences than most other courts in Northern Ireland. The figures may reflect this type of offence, but it should be noted that RUC Incidents figures (see Appendix 1) suggest that domestic violence is very high in Newtownabbey (429 incidents in 1994). A trawl of figures from a wider geographical area, including the West of the province, may be necessary to discern more accurately the true proportion of domestic violence cases in Northern Ireland courts, which may be a higher proportion of all violence offences and of male-female violence than these preliminary figures suggest. We shall return to this point in the conclusion. The figures for Lisburn (domestic violence as 21 per cent of all Offences Against the Person and 82 per cent of male-female offences) would seem to reflect a high prevalence of domestic violence in this area, a finding upheld by RUC Incidents figures, which show a rate of 9.3 per 100,000 population in 1994, the second highest reported incidence rate in the province.

2. It must be stressed that these figures relate to prosecutions. It is acknowledged that domestic violence is a greatly under-reported crime and that only a proportion of those incidents which are reported to the police ever reach the courts. According to Mercer (1993) only slightly less than 12 per cent of cases reported to the RUC in 1991 and 1992 were prosecuted. Therefore the figures presented here cannot by any means be taken to reflect the incidence of domestic violence in the Northern Ireland population which is likely to be considerably higher.

Despite our reservations that the data outlined above are likely to be an under-estimate of the real extent of domestic violence offences as presented at these five courts, we can nonetheless make some tentative conclusions. These are:

- Assaults in general are mostly male to male but a significant section of it is male to female (about one in five cases).

- Of the male to female violence, approximately two-thirds of this is domestic violence.

- Domestic Violence takes up about 14 per cent of the courts' case load of Violence Against the Person (we deal with criminal damage elsewhere).

Sentencing

Table 4.3 presents details of a range of offences for which domestic violence offenders were prosecuted in the five courts, while the graph (page 73) indicates the overall pattern of disposals for domestic violence charges. (Tables for each individual court are presented separately in Appendix 2). Table 4.3 indicates both the number of charges and the number of defendants charged with each offence. It should be noted that the total number of defendants given is greater than the number of defendants cited in Table 4.1. This is because (a) defendants whose sole offence was criminal damage are included in addition to the Offences Against the Person defendants and (b) several individuals appeared on more than one charge, (e.g. threats to kill and AOABH; breach of personal protection/exclusion order and assault, etc).

At the five courts, there was a total of 99 charges, including criminal damage relating to offences of a domestic nature, and of these, 33, or one third, were withdrawn.

In line with figures given by Mercer (1993) in his table of 'Resolution of reported cases to RUC, March 1991-1992', (see page 100) where the 'withdrawal of victim' category accounted for 31 per cent of cases in 1991 (March – Dec) and 39 per cent in 1992, this is a disappointingly high figure and the implications of this withdrawal of prosecution will be discussed in the conclusion.

In discussing sentencing for a range of offences outlined in Table 4.3., first we deal with common assault and then we turn to the more serious assaults. We single out from the more serious assaults Assault Occasioning Actual Bodily Harm (AOABH) since we wish to provide a comparison between the sentencing of domestic violence offenders and other offenders.

Common Assault

The largest single group of charges was for common assault (Section 42): 32 defendants on 36 charges. What is notable here is that as many as half the charges (18 out of 36) were either withdrawn or

TABLE 4.3
Domestic Violence Offences and Sentencing (Five courts)

Offences	No. of Defendants	No. of Charges	Range of Sentencing
Common Assault	32	36	Suspended prison sentence (3) (max. 3 months) Fine (3) (max £100) Conditional discharge (2) Bound over (6) Probation 12 months (2) Adjourned in custody (1) (victim later murdered) To Crown Court on higher charge (1) Withdrawn (13) Dismissed (5)
AOABH	18	18	Fine (4) (range £10-£250) Suspended prison sentence (4) (range 4-9 months) Adjourned (1) Adjourned generally (1) Sent for trial to Crown Court (1) Withdrawn (7)
Criminal damage	18	19	Suspended prison sentence (3) (max 2 months) Fine £100 Fine £50 and compensation (2) Conditional discharge and compensation (6) Compensation order (1) Withdrawn (5) (1 defendant sentenced on other charges and 1 defendant fined £10 for resisting arrest)
Breach of PP/EO	11	13	Suspended prison sentence (7) (range 1-6 months) Fine (2) (£10, £50) Fine and compensation (£50 fine) Conditional discharge (1) Dismissed (2)
GBH W/I & GBH5		6	Withdrawn (4) (1 later tried as assault – withdrawn and 1 to Crown Court on other charges) Adjourned in custody to Crown Court (1)
Threats to kill	4	4	Absolute discharge (1) 6 months suspended prison sentence (1) Withdrawn (2)
Attempted murder	2	2	To Crown Court (1) Withdrawn (1)
Wounding W/I	1	1	Withdrawn (later tried as AOABH) (1)
Total	91	99	

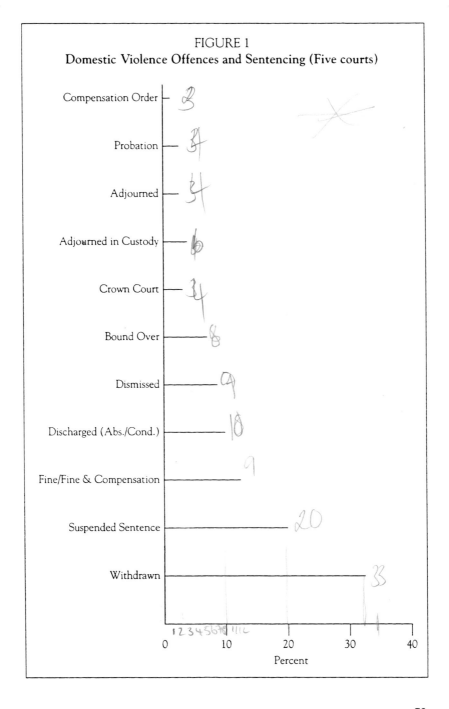

FIGURE 1
Domestic Violence Offences and Sentencing (Five courts)

dismissed. However, in a small number (4) of these cases, the defendants were convicted on other charges such as breach of peace. (For a breakdown by individual courts, see Appendix 2).

Of those defendants who were convicted and sentenced none received an immediate custodial sentence. Three received a suspended prison sentence (maximum three months) and three were fined (maximum £100). Two were given 12 months probation, six were bound over and two received a conditional discharge. It is possible that magistrates regard common assault in a domestic context as none too serious an offence, yet our two randomly selected case studies A and B below, as well as two cases from Bangor Court, illustrate just how serious it is. One defendant on an assault charge at Bangor was also charged with attempted murder of his partner and sent to the Crown Court for trial. Another was remanded in custody, and the case adjourned to a different court. Six months later, according to information from the RUC, the victim of this assault was murdered. The same assailant has since been tried and convicted of manslaughter. This case should alert those involved with criminal justice that domestic common assault may be part of an escalating spiral of potentially lethal violence.

Other Charges

Other charges, from the most to least frequently occurring, included criminal damage; Assault Occasioning Actual Bodily Harm (AOABH) (discussed below); breach of personal protection and exclusion orders (discussed separately in Chapter 5); and other serious charges up to and including attempted murder.

A total of 12 defendants appeared on charges of grievous bodily harm (GBH), wounding, threats to kill and attempted murder. Considering the seriousness of these charges and the terror they must have instilled in the female victims, it is disturbing to note that eight defendants had charges against them withdrawn at their court appearance, although three of these later faced substitute charges: the defendant on the wounding charge was later tried and convicted of AOABH (see case study C, page 90); the defendant originally charged with GBH was sent to the Crown Court for trial on other charges of AOABH and indecent assault; and another charge of GBH was substituted at a later date with an assault charge, though this was also withdrawn. No information is available as to why the other serious

CASE STUDY A

Charges: Two counts of Common Assault

> In the early hours of the morning, the victim was punched on the back of the head, knocked to the ground, then kicked on the legs and slapped on the head. She was pulled along the bedroom floor by the legs. Police entered the house and caught the assailant standing over the victim, who was on her hands and knees. He was holding her by the hair and punching her on the head. Her injuries included bruising to her upper and lower arms, shoulder, elbow, right upper leg and both sides of the lower abdomen, as well as grazes to both knees and a tender scalp.

Defendant pleaded guilty.
Sentence: Three months imprisonment, suspended two years (concurrent)

CASE STUDY B

Charges: 2 counts of Common Assault

> The victim was thrown against the wall of the lounge, thrown on to the settee and punched in the stomach. She was pulled to the floor and kicked in the stomach. Two days later, the assailant slapped the victim about the face. Her injuries were bruising to forearms, legs and pelvic area.

The defendant pleaded not guilty and the victim withdrew her evidence.
Outcome: charges withdrawn.

charges, including one of attempted murder, were withdrawn. Possibly some of these cases were tried on lesser charges at a later date outside the six-month period chosen for research. It is equally possible that the cases collapsed because for some reason, the victim did not cooperate with the prosecution process by giving evidence. If this is the case, further research is needed to investigate the reasons for lack of victim confidence in the criminal justice system in such serious cases and to determine how best to support victims through to

successful prosecution. In the United States, Canada and Australia, Victim Witness Support Programmes have been introduced in order to tackle this problem. These programmes operate from the prosecutor's office and have led to a much higher rate of successful prosecutions. Although Victim Support have received funding to pilot a number of schemes in Britain, the fact that these are separated from the prosecution system may mean that not only will they receive fewer resources but that they are not taken as seriously as the support programmes operated by the prosecutors themselves. Given the fear of intimidation which victims of domestic violence experience and the additional fear of further assaults and retaliation, serious consideration needs to be given to the introduction of such programmes in the United Kingdom.

Of the defendants on serious charges who were dealt with by the courts (and not discussed above), one received an absolute discharge and another a six-months suspended prison sentence for threats to kill (see case study D). Two defendants were sent for trial to the Crown Court on charges of attempted murder and of Grievous Bodily Harm and Wounding With Intent. It seems surprising that only three defendants on these very serious charges were committed for trial to the higher court.

CASE STUDY C

Charges: 1 Possession of offensive weapon
            2 AOABH

This defendant had originally appeared on a wounding with intent to cause GBH charge. This charge was withdrawn and replaced by the above charges 3 months later.

In the early hours of the morning, the victim was walking along the street, when her ex-boyfriend jumped her from behind, pulled her to the ground, punched and kicked her. He put a knife to her neck and threatened her. She sustained cuts to her right eye and to her chin and abrasion to the eyebrow.

The defendant pleaded not guilty.

Sentence: 1 3 months imprisonment, suspended 2 years
            2 9 months imprisonment, suspended 2 years

CASE STUDY D

Charges: 1 Threats to kill
           2 AOABH

The victim was punched, kicked, beaten and a kitchen knife held to her throat while the assailant sat astride her. He threatened to kill her. She sustained bruising to her body, hands, arm, wrist and thigh. She had a small cut to the left ear and the side of her face was tender.

The defendant pleaded guilty. The victim withdrew her evidence but the police proceeded due to the other evidence available.

Sentence: 6 months imprisonment, suspended for 3 years (2) (concurrent)

It has not been within the scope of this report to make a systematic comparison of the treatment of domestic violence offenders with all other types of violent offenders across the whole range of offences. However, in the case of one specific offence, AOABH, an attempt at a comparison of sentencing patterns has been made. We now turn to this issue of the equity in sentencing.

A Comparison in Sentencing of Domestic Violence and non-Domestic Violence Related Offences under Assault Occasioning Actual Bodily Harm (AOABH)

At the five courts, 74 men were prosecuted on this charge for attacks on other men (male-male group), as against 18 domestic violence offenders (domestic violence group). Table 4.4 shows the numbers from each of these groups tried at each court.

TABLE 4.4
AOABH Offenders, January-June 1994 (5 Courts)

	Bangor	Coleraine	Downpatrick	Lisburn	Newtownabbey
Male/Male	16	21	14	8	15
Domestic Violence	4	2	8	2	2

Although the number of domestic violence offenders is clearly much smaller than the male-male group, comparison of sentencing

is at least indicative of differing outcomes for the two groups of offenders. Table 4.5 analyses the pattern of disposals.

TABLE 4.5
Prosecution Outcomes for AOABH

	Male-Male		Domestic Violence	
	No.	%	No.	%
Immediate Custody	7	10	0	0
Suspended Custody	18	24	4	22
Fine	27	36	4	22
Community Supervision	4	5	0	0
Conditional discharge	2	3	0	0
Committed to Crown Court	5	6	1	5
Adjourned	0	0	2	10
Dismissed	3	4	0	0
Withdrawn	8	11	7	39
Total	74		18	

In discussing the above figures, it may be useful first to make a comparison with the 1994 figures for non-scheduled[4] Violence Against the Person Offences. Comparing tables 4.5 and 4.6, it will be noted that for the disposals of immediate custody and community supervision and in rates of dismissal and withdrawal of charges, our figures for the AOABH male-male group by and large match those for the 1994 non-scheduled Offences Against the Person figures for cases appearing at Magistrates Courts. There are however some differences in respect of suspended custody and fines. The domestic violence figures in Table 4.5 are similar to those in Table 4.6 (Magistrates Courts) only in respect of fines; otherwise the figures in the two tables do not compare and this is because the domestic violence figures are skewed by the high proportion of withdrawals of charges (39% domestic violence as against 11% male-male AOABH and 11% for overall non-scheduled Offences Against the Person).

---

4   A non-scheduled offence is the term used to describe an offence not arising from the political situation in Northern Ireland

TABLE 4.6
Prosecution outcomes for violence against the person (non-scheduled) Northern Ireland, 1994 All Courts

Disposal	Magistrates Courts		Crown Courts		All Courts	
	N	%	N	%	N	%
Immediate Custody	231	(13%)	95	(38%)	326	(16%)
Suspended Custody	315	(17%)	78	(32%)	393	(19%)
Fine	466	(25%)	8	(3%)	474	(23%)
Community Supervision	122	(7%)	15	(6%)	137	(6%)
Conditional discharge/ Absolute discharge	122	(7%)	2	(1%)	124	(6%)
Committed	234	(13%)	–	–	234	(11%)
Adjourned	–	–	–	–	–	–
Dismissed[1]	97	(5%)	46	(19%)	143	(7%)
Withdrawn	201	(11%)	2	(1%)	203	(10%)
Other[2]	43	(2%)	1	–	44	(2%)
No	1,831		247		2,078	

1   Includes dismissed, dismissed sine die, nolle prosequi, acquitted, not guilty
2   Includes absolute discharge, bound over, no order, compensation, restitution

If we return to a comparison of the two groups of AOABH offenders in the five courts under study, it is notable that seven (10 per cent) of the male-male group were given an immediate prison sentence, whereas none of the domestic violence offenders were.[5] Only the proportions of those given a suspended prison sentence of up to nine

5   Three of these sentences for male to male violence under AOABH were varied or dismissed on appeal.

months (24 per cent male-male; 22 per cent domestic violence) and of those returned for trial to the Crown Court (6 per cent male-male; 5 per cent domestic violence) are similar.

If we examine fining as a disposal in more detail, differences again emerge between the two groups. Thirty-six per cent (27) of the male-male group were dealt with by means of a fine as against 22 per cent (4) of the domestic violence group. Twenty-four of the 27 men in the male-male group received fines of £100 or more and several were in the region of £250; one was for £450. Only one of the domestic violence offenders received a substantial fine (£250 at Newtownabbey); the three other fines were £10, £50 and £75. At Coleraine, for the male-male offenders, the magistrate combined some suspended sentences with £100 fines or combined fines with compensation to the victim of £100 plus costs, which can be compared with the £10 fine to a domestic violence offender at this court.[6]

Community Supervision as a disposal was not used for domestic violence offenders (either for AOABH or any other domestic violence offence). This is worth noting in the context of enabling these offenders to be directed to an abusers' programme following the prosecution. More specifically if magistrates were to make it a condition that these offenders attend the Men Overcoming Violence programme currently being run by the Probation Service, then some thought needs to be given as to which of the disposals this would be attached.

Conclusion

This study of records of criminal offences at five Magistrates Courts in Northern Ireland shows that on average 14 per cent of all prosecutions for Offences against the Person and 64 per cent of prosecutions for violence by men against women before these courts is domestic violence related. For a number of reasons, however, this may be an under-estimate of the proportion of domestic violence cases prosecuted in Northern Ireland as a whole. A total of 67 domestic violence defendants appeared on Offences against the Person charges and 10 on criminal damage charges. Of these 77

---

6   A note on the court record revealed, however, that the recipient of the £10 fine had spent some time on remand in custody.

defendants, 75 were male and two female, illustrating again that in Northern Ireland as elsewhere, domestic violence is overwhelmingly a crime perpetrated by men against women.

Ninety-nine charges were brought and the vast majority of defendants were dealt with summarily. By far the largest group of charges (36 per cent) related to common assault. Thirteen per cent of charges were for breach of personal protection/exclusion order, 19 per cent for criminal damage and 18 per cent for AOABH. The remainder (13 per cent) were serious charges of GBH Wounding With Intent and GBH, wounding, threats to kill and attempted murder.

Overall, there was a 33 per cent rate of withdrawal of charges. With regard to one specific charge, AOABH, a comparison of domestic violence offenders with another group of offenders, males who attacked other males, revealed that the withdrawal rate for domestic violence defendants on this charge was 39 per cent as against only 11 per cent for the male-male group. We are concerned by this high overall rate of withdrawal for domestic violence offences, particularly in relation to the more serious offences, and its possible implications for continuing and escalating violence. It is clear that methods need to be found to enhance victim confidence in the criminal justice system and to support victims through to successful prosecution, so that domestic violence can be dealt with by the courts in the same way as other crimes of violence.

Another problematic area is the designation of charges and an apparently greater leniency of sentencing for domestic violence offenders. Of the 77 defendants in this study, of those whose cases were not adjourned or sent for trial to a higher court, none received a more severe penalty than a suspended prison sentence (maximum nine months) or fines ranging generally from £10-£100 (one fine of £250 was exceptional). No defendant was given an immediate prison sentence or community service. The AOABH comparison group of male-male offenders were treated more severely, especially in regard to level of fines and immediate custody, than were the domestic violence group. Clearly, some serious charges are withdrawn and brought back to court on a lesser charge, thereby securing a prosecution but also a lighter sentence. It is also possible that some charges of common assault might be more appropriately tried as AOABH. It is not known how many domestic violence cases might be subsumed under breach of the peace charges.

While we appreciate that the sentencing of domestic violence offences is a sensitive and complex area, posing dilemmas for magistrates who may fear that the victim as well as the offender is penalised by heavy fines and custodial sentences (Craig 1992), it is also important that the judicial process takes account of the chronic and potentially lethal nature of domestic violence, by reference to the offender's previous record. Magistrates need to be alert to a previous history of domestic violence and to prioritise the safety of the victim. More wide-ranging and innovative practices for dealing with domestic violence offenders in Northern Ireland should now be explored, including the expansion within the Probation Service of challenging programmes to which perpetrators can be referred by the courts.

FIVE

The Civil Law: Personal Protection and Exclusion Orders

For a number of years, domestic violence victims in Northern Ireland have been able to apply to the courts for protection against violent partners under Article 18 of the Domestic Proceedings (NI) Order 1980 and the Family Law (Miscellaneous Provisions) (NI) Order 1984. Most applications for personal protection and exclusion orders are heard in the Magistrates Courts, where interim (or emergency) orders can be expeditiously granted for a period of up to five weeks, at which time a summons is also issued for a full order hearing. Full personal protection orders can be granted with no expiry date but are normally made for a fixed term of two years,[1] while exclusion orders cannot exceed six months.

In this section we start by presenting the number of orders which are made annually. This gives us some idea of the extent of domestic violence in Northern Ireland.[2] Following these figures, we provide a number of case studies which outline the kinds of circumstances which lead women to seek protection orders. Then we turn to a more in-depth analysis of personal protection and exclusion orders. We look at both emergency and full orders and outline the reasons which might explain the number of repeat orders. We also look at what happens when these orders are breached. In order to provide a profile and pattern of usage in relation to these orders, we analyse the data collected at Bangor, Lisburn and Downpatrick courts. When we discuss the breaches of civil orders we use information from a total of seven courts. But before we go to these individual courts, we turn first to the wider picture for Northern Ireland. Table 5.1 shows the number of personal protection and exclusion orders, both interim and full, made in Northern Ireland in the years 1991 to 1994.

---

1   There are exceptions to this. For example at one court (Coleraine) personal protection orders were normally made for a six month period.

2   In the absence of a Northern Ireland Crime Survey analysis on this issue, this is one of the few sources of information on the extent of domestic violence in Northern Ireland.

TABLE 5.1
Personal Protection and Exclusion Orders 1991–1994

| Year | Personal Protection | | Exclusion | | Total | Total |
	Interim	Full	Interim	Full	PP	EO
1991	1582	918	1535	837	2500	2372
1992	1800	1029	1764	929	2829	2693
1993	1962	1001	1954	968	2963	2922
1994	2190	889	2141	836	3079	2977

Source: Northern Ireland Court Information Service

While there has been some fluctuation in the numbers of full orders granted, the numbers of interim orders granted by the Northern Ireland Courts have continued to rise. In terms of the total numbers of orders made (interim and full), there has been a 23 per cent rise in personal protection orders and an almost 26 per cent rise in exclusion orders between 1991 and 1994. Despite the increase in applications, there has been a decrease in the proportion of full orders in relation to interims.

The civil legislation is being used extensively in Northern Ireland with just under 3,000 orders being issued annually over the past four years. As the rate of increase suggests, the use of both emergency and full orders is likely to continue and will most likely surpass the 3,000 level as more victims become acquainted with, or informed about, their legislative rights. What these figures cannot tell us is whether confidence has grown in the effectiveness of these orders or whether domestic violence is less likely to be tolerated, leading more victims to come forward and make use of the system. Clearly the figures point to the need for such an appraisal. Victim confidence in the civil, as well as the criminal, justice system is an important issue in the field of domestic violence and until this appraisal is undertaken many questions remain unanswered. However, in the absence of this, we outline some of the reasons why women seek protection from the state through civil legislation.

Circumstances Surrounding Personal Protection and Exclusion Orders

Notes taken from affidavits attached to orders kept at one of the courts visited in the course of this research give an indication of the degree of violence and intimidation endured by some women and children in their own homes:-

Woman A tells of being hit with a blunt hatchet and a clock. Now separated from her husband, she suffers health problems as a result of his violence, including anxiety and a terror of going out of the house, even to the shops, in case she should meet him.

Woman B describes how her child was showered with glass from a window broken by a brick thrown by her husband, then later attacked as she held the child in her arms. Having fled to a refuge, she now wishes to return with her child to the family home, but only if her husband is excluded from it.

Woman C reports that she has suffered years of abuse and nervous tension. After a severe beating one night, she feared for her life and fled to a relative's house in her nightclothes.

Woman D, a mother of three children under the age of 5, describes the terror and distress of her children when she was badly beaten by their father.

Woman E, a separated wife applying for a repeat exclusion order, reports intimidation by her husband in the form of slashed tyres and other damage to her car and an actual physical attack on her, all of which took place after the expiry of the previous order.

Woman F describes how her husband became enraged when he found he had no clean shirt for work. He grabbed and pushed her and dragged her on the floor, shouting abuse. Later, he squeezed her round the neck whilst she was nursing their youngest child. She ran to neighbours for help. She has tried to be patient and understanding of his behaviour and to 'sit it out', since his relatives have promised that they would obtain psychiatric help for him, but he refuses to cooperate. She is now terrified of his behaviour.

Woman G, a common-law wife, recounts how on an earlier occasion, her partner had wrecked the house and assaulted her, causing a head injury. The police were called, but he persuaded her to with-

draw charges. She did not know at that time that he had an existing suspended prison sentence. After she took him back, arguments and intimidation continued, particularly after she became pregnant. In the incident which precipitated her request for personal protection and exclusion orders, her partner had locked her in a bedroom for several hours, shouting abuse at her. He had then attacked her and stripped her of her clothes. She felt that rape had only been averted by the screams of her young son. She locked herself and her son in the child's bedroom and next morning called the police, who removed the respondent.

The case of *woman H* illustrates the difficulty for women in obtaining orders on the grounds of mental rather than physical abuse. Pregnant with her sixth child, she reports enduring severe and humiliating verbal abuse from her husband, in front of the children. She states that the children (all under 10) are very upset and she herself is in a state of extreme anxiety. Despite medical evidence from her GP, expressing concern for the health of both mother and baby, this application was dismissed.

Analysis at the Court level

The figures given in Table 5.1 relate only to the numbers of personal protection and exclusion orders (PP/EOs) granted but do not give an indication of how many individuals are involved each year, or of the gender of applicants nor the numbers refused. There is a marked discrepancy between the numbers of interim orders and full orders and it is not known how many individuals who receive interim orders go on to obtain full orders. Furthermore, at each court, a number of applicants may be granted more than one interim order, but the statistics do not reveal how many.

In an attempt at some elucidation of these matters, civil record books for 1994 were examined at three of the courts visited in the course of this research: Bangor, Downpatrick and Lisburn. The information presented below is indicative only and is limited by both the time constraints of the research period and by some lack of uniformity in the way records of personal protection and exclusion orders are kept at each court.[3]

3   More interim and full orders at each court were counted by the researchers than are given in the official NI Court Service Statistics. Court officials attributed the discrepancy to the sheer volume of statistical material, on this and many other matters, that has to be returned.

At this court, 95 interims (either personal protection or exclusion orders or both) were counted. Nine women each obtained two interim orders and four of these went on to obtain full orders. One withdrew at the full order hearing and there was no record of a full order granted to the other four in 1994.

Of the full orders, 92 hearings were scheduled to be heard at Bangor court in 1994; 39 cases were withdrawn and seven were struck out. In other words 50 per cent (46) did not make it to a hearing. Of the 50 per cent (46) which were heard, 44 full orders were granted and two were dismissed. This means that 95 per cent of the cases which made it to a hearing at Bangor court were successful. Almost two thirds of those seeking full orders (28 cases) had recent interim orders pointing to the fact that victims had sufficient confidence in the system to pursue longer term protection.

Lisburn

96 interim orders were counted. Ten individuals each had obtained two (and in one case, three) interim orders and six of these went on to obtain full orders. One women withdrew at the full order hearing but was granted another interim order four weeks later.

One hundred and five cases were scheduled for full orders. Fifty seven of these were granted at this court in 1994, with three cases being dismissed. Again there is a high success rate (95 per cent) for those cases that make it to a hearing. Twenty-four applications for full orders were withdrawn, 19 were struck out and two were marked 'not served' or 'no appearance'. Once again, a high proportion (44 per cent) of the cases scheduled for a full order do not make it through to a court hearing. Over half of the applicants obtaining a full order (32 out of 57) had previously held interim orders.

It is worth noting that at Lisburn, three women were granted repeat full exclusion orders within the year and seven had full personal protection and/or exclusion orders in 1993 also. Clearly the fact that an exclusion order operates for six months only means that these women have had to return to the court within a short period of time. The issue of extending the duration of exclusion orders has been debated for some time both by family law solicitors as well as

by the magistrates in the domestic proceedings courts. Both are aware of the problems which can arise when, after six months, if the exclusion orders are not renewed they become ineffective. Recommendations have been forwarded to the Office for Law Reform for a reconsideration of this time period or alternatively that it be left to magistrates' discretion to decide an appropriate time scale for these orders.

Downpatrick

Sixty eight interim orders were counted. Eight women obtained two or more repeat interim orders, four of whom went on to obtain full orders. Overall, 15 of those holding interim orders went on to obtain full orders.

At this court, there were 56 cases processed for full order hearings. Again a high number (31) were withdrawn and this continues the pattern of more than half of all cases schedules for a full order (55 per cent) not proceeding to a court hearing. Twenty three full orders (including two exclusion orders within the year to one individual) were granted and two were struck out. Of those that are left after the high withdrawal, there was a high success rate; this time of 92 per cent. Overall then some questions are raised by this pattern of a high withdrawal rate from full order hearings, particularly in the light of the success rate for those that do make it through to a court hearing.

Repeat Orders

With regard to the number of repeat interim orders at the Magistrates Courts, interviews with court officials, magistrates, summons servers and a solicitor suggested the following reasons for this occurrence:

- Orders are not effective unless served personally on the respondent. When each order is made, the magistrate states whether it is to be served by a civil summons server or the RUC (depending on the geographical area or the degree of violence involved in the case). Sometimes the summons servers are unable to locate the respondent at the address given by the applicant or at his place of work. If they fail to serve both the interim order and the summons for the full hearing, within 48

hours, it is then the responsibility of the RUC to serve both. Nevertheless, in a perusal of records of Personal Protection/ Exclusion Orders at Belfast Magistrates Court for January-March 1995, we found a 15 per cent failure to serve. In these cases, a further interim order may be made at a later date.

- Solicitors may ask for a full order hearing to be adjourned, pending, say, further reports on custody or maintenance matters and a further interim order is made to cover the gap.

- Women may not appear at a full order hearing, perhaps because of a reconciliation or of intimidation by the partner and the case is withdrawn or dismissed. However, if the violence continues, the woman may need to apply for another interim order at a later date in the same year.

Discrepancy between numbers of interim and full orders

It may be that magistrates are more willing to grant interim orders on an emergency basis on the applicant's evidence alone, but there are also cases where a respondent contests the case at full hearing and a full order is not granted.

In some cases, applicants may feel that an interim order in itself is effective in stopping the violence, because it conveys a strong message from the court to perpetrators that their behaviour is not acceptable.

Sex of applicants

The fact that it is overwhelmingly females who make use of civil legislation to protect themselves against domestic violence is underlined by the very small number of male applicants for Personal Protection and Exclusion Orders noted at the three courts: out of the 512 cases processed for hearings at these courts in 1994 only nine men pursued orders. Of these nine, three were cross-petitions by men; in these cases, both husband and wife petitioned for a full order but both withdrew. They formed part of the seven cases processed for interim orders, of which four were successful. Of the two who pursued full orders, one was dismissed and one was success-

ful. The main point to note here is that the proportion of men pursuing orders out of the total domestic proceedings case load at these three courts is very low, just 1.7 per cent for the study year.

It may be the case that male victims of domestic violence are reluctant through ignorance, embarrassment or shame to make use of the courts for protection. However, a Belfast magistrate noted (May 1995) that he had recently and within a short period granted interim orders to three male applicants, which may be an indication of changing attitudes.

Marital status

At two courts, Lisburn and Downpatrick, information was collected on the marital status of applicants. At Lisburn, of 96 interim orders, 70 (73 per cent) were granted to married applicants, and 46 out of 57 (77 per cent) full order recipients were married to the respondent. At Downpatrick, the figures were 42 out of 68 (62 per cent) for interim orders and 15 out of 23 (65 per cent) for full orders. At these two courts, the majority of civil protection orders were granted to married women rather than co-habitees. This is of course a very small sample, but is likely to be replicated in other courts in Northern Ireland, given that co-habitation is less common here than in other regions of the UK (*Regional Trends* 1994).

To summarise, the number of personal protection and exclusion orders granted by Northern Ireland courts has been steadily rising in recent years, reaching a peak of around 3000 in 1994, which represents an increase of 26 per cent since 1991. The analysis of civil orders at three Magistrates Courts has shown that applicants are overwhelmingly female and the likelihood is that most are married women.

The official court statistics relate to numbers of orders granted but this research indicates that a somewhat smaller number of individuals may be involved, since some applicants obtain repeat interim orders in any one year. For a variety of reasons, the number of interim orders exceeds the number of full orders granted but an implication may be that women are using the legislation effectively to deter further violence. Only further research, based on a wide sample of women who have used the civil courts, will unravel the complexity of issues pertaining to civil protection orders and their

effectiveness. We now turn to what happens when personal protection and exclusion orders are breached.

Breaches of Personal Protection/Exclusion Orders

This section of the report examines the prosecution and sentencing of breaches of civil personal protection and exclusion orders at seven Magistrates Courts. The courts used to collect information were Belfast, Bangor, Coleraine, Downpatrick, Lisburn, Newtownabbey and Newtownards. Most of these cover urban areas but at least four of them have large rural hinterlands. For a period in 1992 and 1993, following the judgement of Judge Petrie that breaches of these orders should be treated as matters for civil action by the victim, rather than being prosecuted by the police, as hitherto, separate records of these civil cases were kept in seven Northern Ireland courts. The researchers were informed by the Northern Ireland Court Service that these courts were: Bangor, Coleraine, Downpatrick, Lisburn, Newtownabbey and Newtownards. Consequently, records at these courts were examined to determine the number of civil cases of breach of an order and the response of the courts to these occurrences.

At five of the courts (all except Newtownards) where daily court order books were also studied to establish the number of domestic violence criminal offences in a six-month period, January-June 1994 (see Chapter 4), breaches of Personal Protection/Exclusion Orders were extracted, since by this period, breach of an order was once again treated as a criminal offence. The information thus gathered is presented in full in the tables below. The Domestic Proceedings Court at Belfast Magistrates' Court has also kept a record of civil and some criminal breaches of personal protection and exclusion orders since 1991. An analysis of this record is also included in this section but is presented and discussed separately, as it covers a different time period.

There was a total of only 44 cases of breaches of personal protection or exclusion orders recorded at the six other courts (that is excluding Belfast). Columns 2 and 3 deal with the cases which were prosecuted by the victim through a solicitor following the Petrie judgement. There were 32 of these cases in the *civil records for 1992 and 1993* at Bangor, Coleraine, Downpatrick, Lisburn,

Newtownabbey and Newtownards. Columns 4 and 5 refer to those cases which were prosecuted following a change in the legislation which made breaches of these orders a criminal offence. There were 12 of these in the *criminal records for the first half of 1994* at Bangor, Coleraine, Downpatrick, Lisburn and Newtownabbey.

TABLE 5.2
Breaches of Personal Protection and Exclusion Orders at Six Courts: Number of Prosecutions

Court	Civil		Criminal	
	Dates	No.	Dates	No.
Bangor	1992-93	Nil	1/1-30/6/94	Nil
Coleraine	5/5/92-1/6/93	8	1/1-30/6/94	4
Downpatrick	1992	2	1/1-30/6/94	3
Lisburn	16/1/92-12/8/92	6	1/1-30/6/94	3
Newtownabbey	2/7/92-6/9/93	10	1/1-30/6/94	2
Newtownards	5/3/92-7/1/93	6	1/1-30/6/94	N/A
Total	1992-1993	32	1/1-30/6/94	12

All defendants were male. The number of prosecutions appears low, given the number of interim and full orders granted at each of these courts in these years (see Table 5.3 below). For example there were no cases, either of a civil or criminal nature, found at Bangor Court and only two civil cases at Downpatrick, one marked 'no outcome recorded' and the other 'court made no order'.

What interpretation is to be placed on the low number of prosecutions, both civil and criminal for breach of an order in these areas? The most positive reading would be that personal protection and exclusion orders are remarkably effective in protecting women in Northern Ireland from further abuse by their partners and that few men breach them. Available research evidence (Barron, 1990; McWilliams and McKiernan 1993) does not however substantiate such an optimistic conclusion. Further research, based on a wide sample of individuals who have been granted personal protection and exclusion orders, is required, in order to gauge more accurately their effectiveness.

TABLE 5.3
Personal Protection/Exclusion Orders 1992-94: six courts

Year	Bangor Interim		Bangor Full		Coleraine Interim		Coleraine Full		Downpatrick Interim		Downpatrick Full	
	PP	EO	PP	EO	PP	EO	PP	EO	PP	EO	PP	EO
1992	63	65	37	35	115	114	81	76	40	32	21	11
1993	62	62	48	44	106	105	73	66	54	55	21	22
1994	73	71	44	42	120	118	65	54	52	50	17	15

Year	Lisburn Interim		Lisburn Full		Newtownabbey Interim		Newtownabbey Full		Newtownards* Interim		Newtownards* Full	
	PP	EO	PP	EO	PP	EO	PP	EO	PP	EO	PP	EO
1992	52	52	45	46	163	154	76	73	76	76	56	50
1993	65	63	53	54	169	162	73	63	107	103	44	46
1994	83	82	50	55	188	181	67	54	147	142	56	55

* includes Castlereagh

Another possible explanation is a reluctance by both victims and police to prosecute breaches: in the case of victims not pursuing cases, fear of retaliation or a lack of confidence in the court system are important factors whilst in the case of the police, a failure to take the offence seriously, or concerns about evidence feature strongly. A small number of senior police officers who were interviewed in the course of this research expressed concerns that their ability to deal with breaches of personal protection and exclusion orders was hampered by the lack of a power of arrest, though in reality this power does exist, however there are some recent signs that the offence is being treated more firmly. The Domestic Violence Liaison Inspector at Bangor, when asked to comment on the absence of any prosecutions at Bangor during the period under scrutiny, reported that there were (in June 1995) three cases pending at this court. The Domestic Violence Liaison Inspector at Lisburn stated that the policy there now is to prosecute all breaches, with or without the support of the victim.

Another factor influencing whether cases reach the court at all may pertain to a perception of magistrates' attitudes to domestic vio-

lence cases. The small number of police officers and magistrates who were interviewed stated that in some cases women had allowed a partner in respect of whom they had an exclusion order to enter the house and that therefore a subsequent complaint of breach of an order was not valid. If such cases do occur, while it is true that some women may not fully comprehend the terms and meaning of an exclusion order, others may be subject to emotional pressure and physical threats to admit the man, and such cases illustrate what may be a difficulty in interpreting evidence in court. This may in turn have a bearing on sentencing, a matter to which we now turn.

Sentencing

Disposals for both civil and criminal breaches of personal protection and exclusion orders at the six courts (Bangor, Coleraine, Downpatrick, Lisburn, Newtownabbey and Newtownards) are combined and presented in Table 5.4. [4]

Disposals

Twenty-four of the 44 defendants (55 per cent) were dealt with by means of a fine (all of the civil cases at Coleraine, eight out ten of civil cases at Newtownabbey and four out of six civil cases at Newtownards). What is notable is the low level of fines imposed, ranging from one fine of £10 for breach of an exclusion order to £100 (in two cases, one a repeat offence). The majority of fines were of a low tariff, in the region of £25-£50. One magistrate, when interviewed, stated his belief that for a defendant living on state benefits, £50 to be paid in ten weeks was a reasonably severe penalty, but presumably not all offenders are unemployed.[5] Three defendants spent time in custody but for very short periods. Two were sentenced to one month's imprisonment but one of these served only 11 days; a third defendant spent one day in custody. (Notes in Court Record) Six offenders (14 per cent of all criminal cases) received suspended prison sentences, generally of one to three months; one defendant's sentence was for six months, suspended for two years, for breach of both personal protection and

---

4   For a breakdown of disposals at each court, see Appendix 3.

5   It is worth noting however that a court social worker reported that court officials would often accept lower repayments of a fine, over a longer period, to avoid default.

TABLE 5.4
Disposal for Breach of Personal Protection/Exclusion Orders: six courts (1992-1994)

Disposals	No. of Cases	Comments
Fine	24	Range £10-£100 1 x £10 1 x £25 1 x £40 + £30 compensation 13 x £40-£50 6 x £75-£80 2 x £100
Suspended prison sentence	6	2 x 1 month 2 x 2 months 1 x 3 months 1 x 6 months
Imprisonment	3	1 x 1 month 1 x 1 day's custody 1 x 28 days (served 11 days)
Conditional/absolute discharge	3	
Withdrawn	1	
Dismissed	2	Pleads not guilty
Discharged Court made no order No outcome recorded Adjourned	5	

exclusion orders, as well as assault. Three defendants were given absolute or conditional discharges and the rest (eight in number) were variously marked in the court record as discharged, dismissed, withdrawn, adjourned, no outcome or 'court made no order'.

Belfast Magistrates' Court

The record kept at the Domestic Proceedings Office at Belfast covered 91 breaches of personal protection/exclusion orders for the

period 1/7/91 – 24/2/95 (only four cases were from 1994 and 1995). See Table 5.5 for a breakdown of disposals in these cases.

TABLE 5.5
Breaches of Interim or Full Personal Protection/Exclusion Orders, Belfast
11/7/91 – 24/7/95: Number of breaches = 91

Disposals	No. of Cases	Comments
Fine	44	Range £5 – £100 1 x £5 16 x £15 – £30 3 x £40 23 x £50 – £60 1 x £100
Imprisonment	5	(1) 28 days (2) 2 weeks; 4 weeks (2 breaches) (3) 4 weeks; 6 weeks (2 breaches concurrent) (4) 2 months (5) 2 months
Suspended Sentence	1	8 weeks, suspended for 2 years
Conditional discharge	1	
Withdrawn	11	
Struck out/dismissed (no appearance)	12	
Arrest warrant issued/ remand on bail	3	
Adjourned	14	
No details of outcome		

---

*   Fine covers more than one offence.

Table 5.6 gives the total numbers of interim and full personal protection/exclusion orders granted at Belfast Magistrates Court

1991-94. Once again, the numbers of prosecutions recorded for breaches of orders seems low in relation to the numbers of orders granted. (However, clearly not all criminal prosecutions for 1994 were included in the Belfast record book.)

TABLE 5.6
Interim/Full Personal Protection/Exclusion Orders at Belfast Court, 1991/94

	Interim		Full	
	PP	EO	PP	EO
1991	341	334	223	212
1992	384	386	220	192
1993	375	377	218	207
1994	392	388	164	144

Forty-four defendants (48 per cent) were given fines, ranging from as little as £5 (one case) up to £100 (one case). Most fines were in the median range £15 – £60. Five defendants were sentenced to immediate custody, the maximum sentence being 2 months. Twenty-three (25 per cent) of the Belfast cases were either withdrawn, struck out or dismissed. It is surprising that at this court, only one defendant received a suspended prison sentence (in 1995). In the remaining cases, defendants were recorded as having been remanded on bail, having an arrest warrant issued against them, having cases adjourned or being given a conditional discharge. In some cases, no details of outcome were recorded.

Conclusion

It seems likely that relatively few cases of breaches of personal protection/exclusion orders ever reach the courts and when they do, they are for whatever reasons dealt with leniently by magistrates, which no doubt has implications for the confidence of police, solicitors and victims in pursuing prosecutions for this offence. Where appropriate, Magistrates should give consideration to stiffer fines and more use of community disposals, such as compulsory

referral to the programmes for perpetrators of domestic violence currently being developed. Given the extent to which police officers are involved in the enforcement of civil orders and in responding to victims of domestic violence where these orders have been breached, we turn finally to the policing of domestic violence in Northern Ireland.

Six

Policing Domestic Violence in Northern Ireland

The role of the police in domestic violence is to protect victims and their children and to enforce the law in relation to the offender's behaviour. In 1991, the RUC in Northern Ireland introduced a Force Order on domestic violence which contained 'a new and more robust policy geared towards arrest and prosecution of offenders'. This policy was accompanied by a set of guidelines which attempted to shift police practice away from an approach which '... smoothed over the dispute and sought reconciliation between the partners'. As part of the implementation of this policy, the RUC introduced a system for recording incidents of domestic violence and for monitoring police practice. More recently, divisional domestic violence liaison officers have been appointed to oversee police response on the ground. As yet, the RUC has not established Domestic Violence Units similar to those described in the literature review, although one such unit is currently being piloted in the West Belfast area.

In Northern Ireland, the 1994 Inspectorate Report commented on the RUC's operational performance with regard to domestic violence. The Inspector found that only a few of the constables that he met were aware of the existence of Domestic Violence Liaison Officers or their responsibilities. He noted improved record-keeping in some subdivisions but regretted that training on domestic violence issues was patchy and had to rely on the commitment of individual supervisors.

Mercer (1993) and Kane (1995) undertook some primary fieldwork as part of post-graduate research on police officers' attitudes to domestic violence, on the exercise of arrest powers, and on the initiation of prosecutions in domestic violence incidents. They have provided the only police data available for Northern Ireland following the 1991 Force Order. This, in itself, points to the need for further evaluations, but in the absence of any published material we turn here to the findings of these two studies.

Mercer's (1993) study comments on police action in the year following the introduction of the policy. He shows that out of the 1552

cases reported to the RUC during 1992, there was an arrest rate of only 11 per cent (Table 6.1). This contrasts to the rate of 24 per cent reported in the West Yorkshire surveys, following the introduction of their policy (see Chapter 2). Of the RUC's 1552 cases, just over one in ten (12 per cent) were prosecuted whilst one-third (35 per cent) had No Further Police Action recorded.

TABLE 6.1
Resolution of Reported Cases to RUC, March 1991 – 1992

	Mar-Dec 1991	%	1992	%
Cases Reported	1448		1522	
Arrest of Offender	150	10.7	175	11.5
Prosecution of Offender	169 (includes 75 by way of charge following arrest)	11.6	180 (includes 78 by way of charge following arrest)	11.8
Withdrawn by victim	445	30.7	596	39.1
Advice and warning to Offender by Police	155	10.7	219	14.3
No further action by Police	679	46.8	527	34.6

Source: Mercer, Unpublished MSc Thesis, University of Ulster, 1993.

* Percentages allow for multiple responses.

Mercer's study (1993) also included a survey of 20 Domestic Violence Liaison Inspectors. He found that only 12 out of the 20 Domestic Violence Liaison Inspectors considered the new policy a success and two of these qualified it as limited. Mercer concludes that his research gives little cheer to those hoping that RUC domestic violence policy had radically changed operational policing of

domestic violence in Northern Ireland. Since many gaps had been left unplugged, he concluded that the police are dealing with domestic violence without the efficiency, uniformity or professionalism aspired to in their policy statement.

Kane's study (1995) is more recent and includes a survey of 83 police officers throughout Northern Ireland who responded to a domestic violence incident during the month of February, 1995. Table 6.2 shows the proportion of assailants who were cautioned, removed, summonsed and arrested in these incidents.

TABLE 6.2
Action as Reported by RUC Officers in the most Recent Incident of Domestic Violence attended in February, 1995

Action	%
Assailant was verbally cautioned	40.2
Assailant was removed	39.0
Assailant was summonsed	14.6
Assailant was arrested	15.9
Total number of incidents	83

Source: Kane, P.(1995) Unpublished, MSc Thesis, University of Ulster.

*   Percentages allow for a combination of responses.

Again, arrest rates are low despite the high level of serious assaults which Kane reports in this study. The reason for this was that the majority of police officers (58 per cent) in the survey still favoured a mediation/counselling approach when dealing with domestic violence incidents and it is of some concern, that most rejected the robust, pro-arrest response outlined in the 1991 Force Order. In particular, those officers with ten years service or more were most likely to favour the non-interventionist style of policing. Kane reports that officers appeared unaware of the assistance which agencies such as Women's Aid could offer and few referrals were made to these agencies. If the police policy is to be effectively implemented on the ground, then this study highlights the urgent need for more

specialised training. Women's Aid comment on the need to have this training adequately resourced, and recommended that the RUC should set aside additional funding to make this possible.

Turning to the victims' response to policing of domestic violence in Northern Ireland, there are three published studies, two of which were undertaken before the introduction of the 1991 Force Order. These are reviewed here in chronological order. The first is by Evason in 1982 who found that 45 per cent of the 155 abused women interviewed in her study had called the police for assistance at some time but their experience indicated that the police response was not simply inadequate but 'a distortion of the law and a denial of the right to protection'. Police officers not only failed to use the powers they had but actually misled women on what they could or could not do in law. Despite serious incidents, some women were told that nothing could be done because it was 'a domestic matter', 'a family matter', 'really nothing to do with the police'.

Kane's study in 1995 found that these attitudes still existed, albeit more discreetly than before. The existence of such attitudes, both now and in the past, increases the possibility that some police officers would side with the man more easily and believe his story. As a result, some women have been led to believe that the only course to take is civil action, pressing charges themselves. However, we have seen already in this report that the belief that domestic violence does not have to be taken as seriously as other crime, or that it is excusable for a man to use violence when provoked is not confined to the police. The approach by the police and prosecutors reflects many conventional social attitudes which will not easily be changed. What is required is a more pro-active response, including training at a variety of levels.

Montgomery and Bell's study in 1986, as its title suggests, deals directly with 'police response to wife assault'. Amongst the 67 women interviewed for this study, two-thirds had called the police, and had done so between one and 30 times. These researchers divided police strategies for dealing with wife assault into four categories:

- in four out of ten cases there was some form of action against the men;
- in one-third of cases no action was taken against the men or an attempt to reconcile the couple had been made;

- in one in ten cases, intervention was a last resort, after other strategies had failed;

- in one in ten cases, an offer of assistance was made to leave the home or to obtain temporary accommodation, but no action had been taken against the assailant.

Even where an intervention strategy was followed, it mostly consisted of removing the man from the house, with no further action being taken. In some cases, the men returned within a short time and repeated the attacks. Where a man was held overnight at the police station, it appeared to be more in response to his behaviour to the police than his behaviour to his wife. In summary, although in 60 per cent of incidents which the police attended, women had been injured and the majority of women asked for some form of action to be taken, in most incidents no such action was taken by the police. Seventy-seven per cent of the women described the police attitude to wife assault as negative and perceived the police to be unsympathetic and unhelpful.

The third study, by McWilliams and McKiernan in 1993, focuses mainly on health and social services issues but gives us an indication of women's experience of the police both before and after the policy was introduced. The researchers found that although 63 per cent, of the sample of 56 women, had contacted the police only 26 per cent had found them helpful. Helpful responses included removing the man from the house, taking the women to a refuge, hospital or relatives, suggesting a solicitor and maintaining a surveillance of the house. One woman praised the action of the police in responding immediately and supporting her in pressing charges; she contrasted this with their inaction prior to the introduction of the police guidelines on domestic violence. However, many more women did not have this positive experience either before or after the 1991 Force Order. Only three women reported that the police had arrested the abuser. Even in 1992, some women reported a 'nothing we can do, it's domestic' attitude. Others said that the police did not believe them, supported the husband or minimised the violence.

This study particularly highlighted the problems of victims of domestic violence in relation to 'the Troubles' in Northern Ireland. Most of the women who reported no police action came from West Belfast and other nationalist areas. As a result of police officers' need to arrange security for themselves, their response time was

slow. Several women waited all night for the police to arrive and were not informed that they would not be coming, thus precluding them from making alternative safety plans. In some communities, women had reservations about contacting the police for any reason, but also had doubts about enlisting the aid of paramilitaries. The availability of legal and illegally held guns in Northern Ireland is another dimension adding to the threat to domestic violence victims. A few women reported that the police would not remove their husbands' guns from the house. During the seventeen months post-ceasefire some of these issues had been resolved, with police officers in previously vulnerable areas reporting a response time of four minutes to domestic violence incidents. However, police response to domestic violence needs to be continually monitored given the concerns raised above and, in this context, it is worth noting that the force order is now under review.

Drawing from the material in this report, the central features of such a review should emphasise: the overriding duty to protect victims and children; the need to treat domestic violence as seriously as other forms of violence; to be well informed and alert to repetitive assaults on female partners; and to make greater use of powers of arrest. However, it may also be an opportune time to introduce innovative ideas and experiments to discover how best to achieve a higher arrest rate for this offence; though it is important that any such scheme should not damage the welfare of victims of domestic violence. In the literature review (page 26) we refer to what has become known as 'the Streatham experiment' in South London, where formal cautioning has been introduced in an attempt to increase the processing of offences of domestic violence. The number of domestic violence offences which were formally processed by any means, increased substantially and not only did the cautioning rate itself rise, but more incidents were recorded as crimes, arrests were made for more crimed cases and charges resulted for substantially more crimes recorded.

In Northern Ireland, a procedure for 'adult cautioning' exists but it has not been used in domestic violence cases. A formal caution, in contrast to a verbal caution, is recorded on an individual's criminal record and repeat offences can then be monitored. Adult cautions influence sentencing in prosecutions for subsequent offences. Formal cautioning of this nature enables police officers themselves, rather than the victim, to institute proceedings where re-offending

occurs. It can be used in cases where the DPP subsequently direct 'no prosecution'. As such, one might think it is an appropriate police response to incidents of domestic violence particularly where there is a possibility that the victim will discontinue with a prosecution because of her apprehension about such a course of action. Given the requirement that the offender must admit the offence, one might question the extent to which this will happen in domestic violence incidents. On the other hand, if admissions are made, there may also be some concern that the offender may be led to believe that adult cautions are the easy way out. However, clear and reliable admissions might also open the possibility of monitoring future behaviour. What needs to happen in such cases is that the offender receives a clear message that his offending behaviour is unacceptable, it is being recorded as such and should he re-offend, then he will be facing a more serious charge as a result of police action. The police likewise need to receive appropriate training on this innovation, particularly if we wish to avoid the scenario in which formal cautions become the preferred police alternative to court prosecutions. To put it another way, where evidence is sufficiently strong for court prosecutions and the woman is determined to pursue her case, then the case should proceed to a hearing. Where abused women are frightened and/or wish to withdraw from prosecution, and where police officers believe that the charge cannot be sustained in her absence, the offender should receive a formal caution. Should he be found guilty of re-offending, then the evidence of having received the caution will be taken into account in sentencing. In such cases, prosecutors would find less reason to be lenient with men who perpetrate domestic violence and this may help to make offenders realise that their behaviour is less likely to be tolerated in the future.

If formal cautioning were introduced in Northern Ireland, monitoring would also be needed to check if this particular innovation assisted women who had experienced abusive behaviour and increased their confidence in the police. The monitoring of such a scheme should be the responsibility of a senior police officer and the results of the programme should be made public after a set time period such as six or twelve months. Clearly we need more ideas and innovation to devise ways of increasing the processing by the criminal justice system of offences of domestic violence, and it is to these recommendations and interventions that we now turn.

SEVEN

Conclusions and Recommendations

This report shows that fatalities and assaults causing serious injuries in the context of domestic violence are as much a reality in Northern Ireland as anywhere else. Despite how much we would like to believe in democratic and non-violent marriages, the data provided here serve as a reminder that for many women and children the home can be a very dangerous place. The fact that much of the violence is by male partners on women with whom they have currently, or previously had, a relationship can be a difficult thing to accept. This can be as hard for the victims to come to terms with as it is for those working in the criminal justice system. If this behaviour is to be made unacceptable then we must start by recognising that violence in the context of interpersonal relationships is criminal to the same extent as violence in any other context. The material provided here, however, questions whether it is always seen to be so.

In this concluding section, we draw together the main findings and provide the contextual material for a series of recommendations which immediately follow. To date, there has been surprisingly little research on the criminal justice system and domestic violence anywhere in the UK. This may be due to the fact that the statistical evidence for such studies is still relatively poor. For example, in this study it was not possible to assess the level of domestic violence subsumed under common assaults because such cases are not separately recorded or documented. From the jurisdiction of the five magistrates courts included in this study, we found that approximately 14 percent of all Offences Against the Person cases related to domestic violence but a trawl of figures from a wide geographical area may be necessary to discern more accurately the true proportion of reported domestic violence cases in Northern Ireland courts. Since many cases had to be eliminated due to the difficulty in distinguishing domestic violence offences, we believe that there is a higher proportion of all violent offences and male-female violence which is domestic violence related than these preliminary figures suggest. If a framework for collecting crime statistics at both the magistrate and crown court levels was put in place, both legislators

and policy makers would be in a better position to assess the extent to which court time and resources are devoted to domestic violence. It should also provide the necessary information on Breach of the Peace and criminal damage cases related to domestic violence as well as the number of breaches of personal protection and exclusion orders. With this data, we should be better able to monitor the situation in the future. In the absence of this framework, it will remain difficult to document the costs of domestic violence within the criminal justice system.

With improved data sets, it should also be possible to undertake research throughout the United Kingdom on the magnitude of heightened homicide risk and sublethal violence incurred by women who have left relationships. Police statisticians, coroners, and officials working in the court information system could utilise this data to improve practice amongst those tasked with providing protection and safety for separated or divorced people who continue to report persistent abuse from their previous partners. Support services are crucial whilst the relationship is on-going but may become even more so when a women who has been abused threatens to leave. The estrangement itself, and the months immediately following the split up, can lead to an escalation in the life-threatening nature of the assaults which means that this is a particularly dangerous time for abused women and children. Many who seek help at this time do so within this frame of knowledge. Women who report having their lives threatened need to be taken seriously and attended to urgently. Where fatalities can be prevented then the onus is on service providers to put in place the appropriate training and resources to do so.

Recognising that women incur risk of severe violence at separation necessitates action to guarantee their safety. The coercive use of such violence and threats implies more. Men threaten and use violence to constrain women's options and continued failure to acknowledge this constitutes a denial of women's entitlement to autonomy. The effects of violence on women's lives will not be fully understood until the question of the extent to which coercive violence serves the interests of its perpetrators is addressed.

Given the lack of familiarity with the prosecution system, victims of domestic violence deserve to be kept informed about their cases, especially when charges have been reduced. If victim confidence is to be enhanced in the criminal justice system then procedures need

to be introduced which enable prosecutors to explain the various steps taken to ensure a successful prosecution. Those who have been directly affected by repetitive, serious and life threatening assaults need to be better briefed about the preliminary enquiry in relation to their cases; particularly if they wish to have an input into this process. When this does not happen, and when charges are reduced or cases dismissed, then victims can become extremely disillusioned or perceive their efforts to achieve justice to have been wasted. Similarly, those working within the prosecution system should receive specialist training in the area of domestic violence in order to understand the fears and aspirations of victims and to appreciate better the context in which much of this violence takes place.

Also of some concern is the extent to which domestic violence cases are withdrawn from prosecution. We found withdrawal rates of 33 per cent, which is a high figure considering the seriousness of the charges. It is disturbing to note, for example, that eight defendants had charges against them withdrawn at their court appearance, although three of these later faced substitute charges. No information is available as to why the other serious charges, including one of attempted murder, were withdrawn. Possibly some of these cases were tried on lesser charges at a later date outside the six-month period chosen for research. It is also worth noting that during this six month period, the withdrawal rate for domestic violence defendants on the charge of Assault Occasioning Actual Bodily harm (AOABH) was 39 per cent as against only 11 per cent for the male-male group charged with the same offence. Again, it may be that the domestic violence cases collapsed because the victim did not cooperate with the prosecution process by giving evidence. If this is the case, further research is needed to investigate the reasons. It is possible that a reconciliation may have taken place between the time of the initial charge and the time the case eventually comes to court. However, in cases where a reconciliation has not taken place, victims may be reluctant to give evidence because of fear or because they lack confidence in the criminal justice system. We need to determine then how best to support such victims through to successful prosecution. As much as possible should be done to help women who are frightened to go to court and give evidence against their attacker.

It is still the case that some victims of domestic violence receive too little advice on the kinds of support needed to sustain them through the prosecution process whilst others receive too much advice on

how to reconcile. Those engaged in the prosecution system, as well as those involved in work with perpetrators, need to fully take on board the importance of delivering an appropriate level of protection for abused women. Where custodial sentences are given, there should be collaboration in sentence planning from the beginning of the sentence and a more informed exchange of information between the Prison Service and Probation Service in order to prepare the victim for the offender's final release into the community. All organisations will need to work together to develop good practice in dealing with both the victims and the offenders.

Despite the symbolic significance of prosecution, criminal sanctions do not offer a complete solution to domestic violence, or deal adequately with the consequences for those who experience it. Victims need a comprehensive support system which should include independent advice and advocacy services. As Victim Support (1992) comment in their national inter-agency working party report 'Reluctant witnesses may not be very effective witnesses'. If a woman is frightened at the prospect of having her partner convicted and anticipates further violence or intimidation as a result of continuing with the prosecution, then her views about acting as a witness in such cases should be understood in this context. When a woman is left unprotected and unsupported while legal processes take their slow course, it is not surprising that many withdraw in despair from criminal proceedings.

Where the state wishes to retain the support of victims through prosecution, then greater liaison needs to be developed with both statutory and voluntary organisations. If a woman believes herself to be in danger from her assailant in the run-up to a trial, then adequate protection and support must be offered. This might entail the police leaving her in possession of her family home and imposing bail conditions on her alleged assailant such as he could not visit it; or it might entail arranging alternative protected accommodation for her and her children. If magistrates are concerned about removing a woman's means of support when they impose a custodial sentence on her partner, then urgent arrangements should be put in place for alternative income support either through social security or interim financial support from the social services.

Problems such as these have to be faced both in the Crown and Magistrates Courts when the issue of domestic violence arises.

Clearly there is a particular vulnerability where victims of domestic violence are concerned, especially when they are required to go back and live, unprotected, with their assailants. In cases of serious violence, arguments should be put to the court that the man should be remanded in custody because of the likelihood of the offender interfering with the witness. If the prosecution has the right to pursue a case, then the state has the accompanying duty to provide some protection for victims. As Victim Support (1992) note 'every effort should be made such that the crime of domestic violence can be pursued as energetically as any other', and indeed the likelihood of repetition would suggest that domestic violence should be pursued even more rigorously. What is clearly missing from our criminal justice system at present are models for support, consultation and advocacy. Court advocacy for victims of domestic violence is urgently needed and could be based on the good practice models already in existence elsewhere (see Chapter 2). A Domestic Violence Support Programme could be monitored for a period of time to assess its effectiveness in increasing confidence in the judicial process. A domestic violence advocacy scheme could respond to the invitation of a woman who wishes to pursue or assist criminal proceedings but remains concerned about the repercussions of such a course of action. It could support her in her subsequent decisions and might act as a referral point, following community disposals or custodial sentences, to the recently introduced programmes for perpetrators. Such an intervention would help to develop a much more co-ordinated response to victims from police, Women's Aid and other support agencies as well as from those in the legal and judicial system.

Another problematic area is the designation of charges and the apparent leniency of sentencing for domestic violence offenders. It is clear that some serious charges are withdrawn and brought back to court on a lesser charge, thereby securing a prosecution but also a lighter sentence. It is also possible that some charges of common assault might be more appropriately tried as AOABH. In addition to this it is not known how many domestic violence cases might be subsumed under Breach of the Peace charges.

Of the 77 defendants in the five Magistrates Courts under study, of those whose cases were not adjourned or sent for trial to a higher court, none received a more severe penalty than a suspended prison sentence (maximum nine months) or fines ranging generally from

£10-£100 (one fine of £250 was exceptional). No defendant was given an immediate prison sentence. The AOABH comparison group of male-male offenders were treated more severely, especially in regard to level of fines and immediate custody, than were the domestic violence group.

While we appreciate that the sentencing of domestic violence offences is a sensitive and complex area, posing dilemmas for magistrates who may fear that the victim as well as the offender is penalised by heavy fines and custodial sentences, it is also important that the judicial process takes account of the chronic and potentially lethal nature of domestic violence, by reference to the offender's previous record. Magistrates need to be alert to a previous history of domestic violence and to prioritise the safety of the victim. What must be taken much more seriously is that when domestic violence occurs it is rarely a one-off incident. More than any other crime, it is likely to be repetitive and to increase in intensity and frequency as it repeats itself.

In this study, we came across incidents in which defendants had been charged and sentenced, then re-offended and brought back to court on a more serious charge but the penalties of re-offending did not seem to be reflected in the sentencing. Of some cause for concern are the cases of two offenders who had previously been sentenced for serious assaults on their partners and who were eventually prosecuted for murder. These cases should alert those involved with criminal justice that assaults on female partners may be part of an escalating pattern of potentially lethal violence and that this needs to be taken into account when passing sentence.

The number of cases before the courts in Northern Ireland are the proverbial tip of the iceberg. The police deal with many more incidents than are formally prosecuted. Regarding the police, there is a need to constantly consider their powers of arrest and detention in domestic violence cases both because of the experience from other countries of its possible deterrent effect and because of its importance as a means of showing the woman that she is entitled to, and will receive, society's protection and support. Domestic violence units have also be seen to be effective elsewhere and despite the fact that specially designated officers have now been assigned to domestic violence duties in each sub-division, Northern Ireland still does not have any such dedicated units. If Domestic Violence

Units were to be established then they should adopt best practice from elsewhere. These tend to be units which operate under an investigative model, by enabling women to make retrospective statements after the incident and to follow up the high proportion of cases where the perpetrator has either temporarily or permanently left the scene.

One further intervention which should be considered in this context is the procedure of formal cautioning. Monitoring procedures should be set up both to assess its effectiveness and to check if this particular innovation assists the welfare of the victims. What we need is more research and innovation to devise ways of increasing the processing by the criminal justice system of offences of domestic violence. In the short-term, an action-research project could be designed which would appraise the effectiveness of different interventions in different places. For example this could evaluate the impact of arrest and detention procedures in one area, formal cautioning in a second area and court advocacy and victim support in a third. On the other hand, a combination of innovations could be assessed through follow-up interviews with victims in an area where these are being piloted.

These more wide-ranging and innovative practices for dealing with domestic violence offenders should now be explored. The expansion within the Probation Service of challenging programmes to which perpetrators can be referred by the courts should also form part of a more comprehensive response to the problem. These programmes are not to be seen as a diversion from prosecution. They should only be used where a custodial sentence appears unlikely or where the offender has been released on parole. Probation Orders could be used more extensively in these cases to mandatorily direct the perpetrator to the programme. His actions could be monitored for a successive number of months to determine any changes in his behaviour and his partner consulted for her views so as to make a comprehensive assessment of the effectivenes of the programme. All such programmes should have systems for monitoring men's behaviour and the programmes should be independently evaluated.

Despite our focus on the criminal justice system, it is worth noting that those experiencing domestic violence are more likely to seek protection through the civil courts. The official court statistics relate

to the number of personal protection and exclusion orders granted annually, which is approximately 3,000 at present. This research indicates, however, that a somewhat smaller number of individuals may be involved since some applicants obtain repeat interim orders in any one year. We do not know the number which are refused so this figure may underestimate the number of initial applicants. The number of interim orders also exceeds the number of full orders granted and one implication may be that women are using the legislation effectively to deter further violence. A less sympathetic reading may be that they are discouraged from going any further by the trauma of being cross-examined at a court hearing, particularly when confronted by partners contesting full orders. Alternatively, any lack of enforcement of civil orders may lead them to 'drop out' of the system at this stage. Only further research, based on a wide sample of women who have used the civil courts, will unravel the complexity of issues pertaining to civil protection orders and their effectiveness. In the short-term, however, separate waiting facilities for victims would appear to be a pre-requisite for resolving at least one of these issues.

The issue of extending the duration of exclusion orders has also been debated for some time by family law solicitors and by the magistrates in the domestic proceedings courts. Both are aware of the problems which can arise when, after six months, if the exclusion orders are not renewed they become ineffective. Victim support agencies have also recommended that the Office for Law Reform should reconsider this restrictive time period. Some magistrates believe that it should be left to their discretion to decide an appropriate time scale for exclusion orders. The way in which some men continue to use violence, or to stalk their partners, long after the relationship is ended should alert legislators to the need to extend protection for a much longer period of time. Legislation in this field has recently been reviewed by the Office for Law Reform in Northern Ireland. However the proposals to amend the current legislation also fail to address this issue.

Legislation also needs to address the problem that victims of domestic violence are required to provide evidential proof that an assault has taken place before they can use the protection of the civil courts. This remains a major issue not just for those seeking their first exclusion order but also for those who are seeking renewal of their orders. To wait for such an assault to take place is to tempt fate since it could be too late for the order to be of any use. Women who cannot afford for this to happen, may be forced to leave their homes

in order to protect themselves. If civil protection is to mean what it says then this issue has to be taken seriously and extensions to an exclusion order should be granted more generously than is currently the case. Either the Office for Law Reform should take the opportunity to introduce this now or should direct magistrates to use their discretion to extend these orders.

One study, undertaken in the United States, notes that since the introduction of these orders women are less likely to resort to killing their abusive partners (Browne and Williams 1993). The same does not hold for men who kill their wives or girlfriends. In other words the number of female homicide victims has not decreased but the number of male victims has since civil legislation was introduced. We do not know the extent to which this may hold for other countries, particularly since the data on domestic violence homicides have only recently begun to be analysed. From the information which is available, the homicide figures tend to vary from year to year in Northern Ireland, as is also the case elsewhere.

We can make some tentative judgements about the circumstances in which women kill their partners in Northern Ireland from the court proceedings of these cases. Due to their previous history of domestic violence in these murder cases, the women defendants have been found guilty of the lesser charge of manslaughter. In two cases out of seven, the women were acquitted. Elsewhere, cases in which women have received mandatory life sentences for killing abusive husbands have subsequently led to public campaigns and demands to have these convictions and sentences reviewed. A register of the various outcomes of court cases both in Northern Ireland and elsewhere may assist such a review.

Many more women than men are victims of domestic violence homicides. It would appear that where women have been killed as a consequence of domestic violence then a range of mitigating circumstances have been allowed to reduce the charge from murder to manslaughter. When there is strong evidence of persistent domestic violence, then one might question how such circumstances are allowed to mitigate his behaviour. In cases in which mitigation and provocation reflect more the gendered nature of the relationship, then the legal system needs to consider the extent to which it is condoning, rather than condemning, this violence. In particular, the outcomes and sentences involved in the attempted murder cases

reported here may cause some concern to those attempting to provide protection and safety to the victims. The judicial system needs to take the issue of domestic violence much more seriously and it needs to put the story of the assailant and the victim together in a much more coherent way than is the case at present. To do this, it needs to seek advice and expertise from those who work with abused women. They may be able to produce pre-trial reports on the serious, long term effects of domestic violence and to provide a more holistic picture about the kinds of abusive and coercive behaviour leading up to such events. Rather than providing access to prosecution lawyers on the day of the trial, the Department of Public Prosecutions should attempt to involve victims much more at the pre-trial stage, particularly since they are to be their main witnesses. Where women have survived attempts on their lives, this is the least they should expect. In London, Ontario, for example victims have the right to meet the prosecutor within two weeks of a charge being laid (Kelly, 1994).

The expertise of agencies such as Women's Aid should be better utilised by the criminal justice system at all of these stages. Clearly, any co-ordinated response to protection and safety needs to draw on their ability to provide emergency support for abused women and children as well as their knowledge of the kinds of services that are needed to protect women. Women's Aid should be involved in the delivery of training to officials within the judicial system in addition to the training which has been initiated with police officers on the ground. For this to take place effectively, financial resources need to be set aside by these agencies since Women's Aid cannot be expected to deliver these services from within their current budget.

Domestic violence is an 'everyday' crime in Northern Ireland. It can also be extremely dangerous and have very serious consequences for its victims. Too often, women are left in situations where they will be assaulted again, or indeed killed. Such homicides have been highlighted here and point to the need for prosecutors to be alert to the repetitive nature of this crime. Domestic violence is clearly a major social problem and one that needs our urgent attention. Violence in the home must be prevented if we wish to reduce violence in society. Individuals at the policy level have to seek ways to reduce the high levels of serious assaults which take place in the context of domestic violence. Interventions should be found to enable victims, and those working with them, to pursue the kinds of

justice which fit the crime and police officers, prosecutors, policy makers and lawyers have a duty to respond accordingly. As the public awareness campaign states 'when home is where the hurt is,' we need to act now.

Recommendations

Recommendation 1

In order to obtain a more accurate picture of the extent of domestic violence in Northern Ireland, a framework for collecting crime statistics at both the Magistrates and Crown Court levels should be put in place. A coding system for domestic violence cases should be introduced with the on-going computerisation of court records.

Recommendation 2

A register of the various outcomes of domestic violence related murder, manslaughter and attempted murder court cases in Northern Ireland and in Great Britain should be established.

Recommendation 3

The RUC should robustly implement its pro-arrest policy for domestic violence offences. Where police bail is set, the protection of the victim should be paramount.

Recommendation 4

The RUC should continue to develop training on domestic violence issues and set aside financial resources for such training.

Recommendation 5

In light of the high withdrawal rate of domestic violence charges, the RUC should consider the use of formal cautioning (see Chapters 2 and 6). Formal cautioning should not, however, become the preferred police method of dealing with domestic violence cases, as an alternative to court prosecution.

Recommendation 6

More wide-ranging and innovative practices for dealing with domestic violence offenders in Northern Ireland should be explored.

Recommendation 7

The RUC should involve victims more in the preparation of the preliminary enquiry file and keep victims better informed at every stage of the prosecution process. The DPP should offer a rationale to victims or to a deceased victim's family where they have reviewed a charge, leading to a reduced charge, or where they have agreed to accept a plea to a lesser charge.

Recommendation 8

The Judicial Studies Board should include the issue of domestic violence in their training programme for magistrates and judges.

Recommendation 9

Probation officers should make every effort to notify victims of the imminent release of an offender from custody.

Recommendation 10

Professionals should be particularly alert to the increased level of support and protection needed by women in the dangerous period after leaving an abusive relationship.

Recommendation 11

A much more co-ordinated response to victims from the police, voluntary support agencies and the legal and judicial system is required. Where victims volunteer to give evidence, or are compelled to do so, some thought should be given to the provision of a Victim Witness Support Programme, linked to the prosecution system.

Recommendation 12

Further research should be undertaken to assess domestic violence victims' satisfaction with the criminal justice system. This should include a study of the type of compensation awarded for criminal injuries.

Domestic Violence

Total Number of Incidents Attended by Police in 1994 and Comparisons
with 1992 and 1993

	1994	1993	1992
Musgrave Street	11	6	2
Mountpottinger	28	61	33
Donegall Pass	59	88	85
Dunmurry	144	103	70
'A' Division	242	258	190
Grosvenor Road	106	39	49
Woodbourne	87	113	59
Lisburn	60	88	97
'B' Division	253	240	205
North Queen Street	84	52	78
Newtownabbey	429	464	69
Antrim Road	73	71	46
Carrickfergus	91	75	26
Tennent Street	361	157	353
Antrim	54	22	59
'D' Division	1092	841	631
Strandtown	47	365	75
Bangor	39	90	46
Castlereagh	16	19	21
'E' Division	102	474	142
Newtownards	46	89	42
Downpatrick	58	48	61
Newcastle	24	51	36
'G' Division	128	188	139
Armagh	37	47	37
Newry	146	72	82
'H' Division	185	119	119

Table 1 cont'd

Domestic Violence: Total Number of Incidents Attended by Police in
1994 and Comparisons with 1992 and 1993

	1994	1993	1992
Portadown	18	34	26
Lurgan	28	62	92
Banbridge	11	44	34
'J' Division	57	140	152
Cookstown	46	23	24
Dungannon	47	39	28
'K' Division	93	62	52
Enniskillen	64	55	53
Lisnaskea	68	63	31
Omagh	23	50	70
'L' Division	155	168	154
Strand Road	48	150	119
Strabane	76	37	41
Waterside	42	35	45
'N' Division	166	222	205
Coleraine	138	74	75
Limavady	40	51	50
Magherafelt	51	41	40
'O' Division	229	166	165
Ballymena	39	72	45
Ballymoney	45	19	42
Larne	34	49	51
'P' Division	118	140	138
Total – Northern Ireland	2820	3018	2292

Source: RUC Statistics, 1995.

Details of Sentences for Domestic Violence Offfences at each of the Five Magistrates' Courts

Bangor

Offence	No. of Defendants	No. of Charges	Comments
Assault	6	6	Adjourned, remanded in custody (found guilty of manslaughter of female partner on a subsequent charge) Sent for trial to Crown Court on attempted murder charge Conditional discharge, 12 months Prison 3 months, suspended 2 years Dismissed (2)
AOABH	4	5	Prison 4 months, suspended 2 years Withdrawn (but returned for trial at Crown Court on attempted murder and assault charges) Returned for trial at Crown Court (+ other charges) Adjourned on bail and conditions
GBH W/I	1	2	Adjourned to Crumlin Road, remanded in custody
GBH	1	1	Withdrawn (but returned to Crown Court on other charges)
Criminal damage	2	2	Prison 1 month, suspended 2 years Conditional discharge 12 months + compensation
Attempted murder	1	1	Returned for trial to Crown Court

Coleraine

Offence	No. of Defendants	No. of Charges	Comments
Assault	6	6	Withdrawn (2) Dismissed (pleads NG) Probation 12 months Fine £100 Bound over 12 months on £100
AOABH	2	2	Fine £10 (has been held in custody) Prison 6 months, suspended 2 years (has been in custody 3 months)
Disorderly behaviour	2	2	Withdrawn (2) (sentenced on other charges)
Criminal damage	5	6	Withdrawn (sentenced on other charges) Conditional discharge + compensation £1375.70 in 12 weeks Fine £50 + £50 compensation (female defendant) Fine £50 + £60 compensation Fine £100
Breach of PP and/or EO	3	4	Fine £40 + £30 compensation Fine £50 in 8 weeks Dismissed (pleads not guilty)

Downpatrick

Offence	No. of Defendants	No. of Charges	Comments
Assault	6	6	Withdrawn (4) (includes 1 assault on child) Fine £75 + costs Conditional discharge 12 months
AOABH	8	8	Withdrawn (5) Adjourned generally Fine £75 Fine £50
GBH (on child)	1	1	Withdrawn
Threats to kill	3	3	Withdrawn (2) Absolute discharge
Criminal damage	3	3	Withdrawn Conditional discharge 12 months + compensation Conditional discharge 2 years + compensation (female defendant)
Breach of PP and/or EO	3	4	Prison 1 month, suspended 12 months Prison 6 months, suspended 2 years (concurrent) Fine £10

Lisburn

Offence	No. of Defendants	No. of Charges	Comments
Assault	8	12	Prison 3 months, suspended 2 years (on 2 charges) Probation 12 months Bound over 1 year (3) Withdrawn (7) Dismissed
AOABH	2	2	Prison 6 months, suspended 3 years (concurrent) Prison 9 months, suspended 2 years
GBH W/I	1	1	Withdrawn. Remanded and later tried as Assault (withdrawn)
Wounding W/I	1	1	Withdrawn. Later tried as AOABH
Threats to kill	1	1	Prison 6 months, suspended 3 years (concurrent)
Criminal damage	3	3	Prison 1 month, suspended 3 years (concurrent with breach) Withdrawn + resisting arrest – fine £100 Conditional discharge for 2 years (concurrent with breach)
Breaches of PP and/or EO	3	3	Prison 1 month, suspended 3 years Prison 3 months, suspended 3 years Conditional discharge for 2 years

Newtownabbey

Offence	No. of Defendants	No. of Charges	Comments
Assault	6	6	Prison 2 months, suspended 18 months (2) Fine £75 and bound over 12 months on £200 Withdrawn (2) (but bound over 18 months on £100 on breach of peace charge x 2) Dismissed
Attempted murder	1	1	Withdrawn (+ Wounding W/I GBH on son – withdrawn)
GBH	1	1	Withdrawn
AOABH	2	2	Fine £250 Withdrawn
Breaches of PP and/or EO	2	2	2 months prison, suspended 2 years 2 months prison, suspended 18 months
Criminal damage	5	5	Prison 2 months, suspended 18 months Compensation £145.76 or 30 days prison Conditional discharge 12 months + compensation £55 Withdrawn (2)

Disposals for Breach of Personal Protection/ Exclusion Orders: Six Courts

Bangor

Civil cases	None
Criminal cases	None

Coleraine

Civil cases   5.5.92 – 1.6.93

Disposals	No. of Cases	Comments
Fine	8 defendants (9 breaches)	Range £25-£100 1 x £25 5 x £50 1 x £80 1 x £100

Criminal cases: Jan – June 1994

Disposals	No. of Cases	Comments
Fine		(1) £40 + £30 compensation (breach of PP) (2) £50 (breach of EO)
Dismissed	2	(1) Breach of PP/EO and breach of EO (area). Pleads not guilty. (2) Breach of PP. Also assault charge. Pleads not guilty.

Downpatrick

Civil Cases: (2)

Date	Disposal
18/3/92	Arrest 6/4/92. Bailed. No outcome recorded.
16/4/92	Court made no order.

Criminal Cases: Jan – June 1994

Disposals	No. of Cases	Comments
Suspended Prison Sentence	2	(1) 1 month, suspended 12 months (breach of EO) (2) 6 months, suspended 2 years x 3 (for breach of PP, breach of EO, assault)
Fine	1	£10 (breach of EO)

Lisburn

Civil Cases: 16/1/92 – 12/8/93

Disposals	No. of Cases	Comments
Fine	1	£75
Conditional Discharge	1	for 12 months
Absolute Discharge	1	
Withdrawn	1	Full order made
Adjourned	2	

Lisburn

Criminal Cases: Jan – June 1994

Disposals	No. of Cases	Comments
Suspended prison sentence (breach 21/11/93)	2 breaches (1 defendant)	1 month, suspended 3 years (concurrent with sentence for criminal damage)
Suspended prison sentence (breach 25/12/93)		3 months, suspended 3 years
Conditional discharge	1	For 2 years (concurrent with same sentence for criminal damage)

Newtownabbey

Civil cases: 2/7/92 – 6/9/93

Disposals	No. of Cases	Comments
Fine	8	Range £40 – £100 1 x £40 3 x £50 3 x £75 1 x £100 (repeat offence)
Imprisonment	1	1 month
Discharged	1	

Criminal cases: Jan – June 1994

Disposals	No. of Cases	Comments
Suspended Prison Sentence	2	(1) Breach PP/EO and assault 2 months, suspended 18 months (2) Breach PP 2 months, suspended 2 years

Newtownards

Civil cases: 5/3/92 – 7/1/93

Disposals	No. of cases	Comments
Fine (all breaches of PP)	4	Range £40 – £80 2 x £40 1 x £50 1 x £80
Imprisonment	2	(1) 1 day's custody (2) 28 days (court date 5/3/92); Warrant revoked (court date 16/3/92)

Criminal cases:no data collected

Bibliography

BARRON, J. (1990) *Not Worth the Paper...? The Effectiveness of Legal Protection for Women and Children Experiencing Domestic Violence*. Bristol: WAFE.

BOWMAN, C.G. (1992) 'The Arrest Experiments: a Feminist Critique'. *Journal of Criminal Law and Criminology*, Vol. 83, No. 1.

BROWNE, A. (1987) *When Battered Women Kill*. New York: Free Press.

BROWNE, A. and WILLIAMS, K.R. (1993), 'Gender, intimacy and lethal violence: trends from 1976 through 1987. *Gender and Society*, Vol. 7, No. 1.

BUCHAN. L. and EDWARDS, S. (1991) *Adult Cautioning for Domestic Violence*. London: Police Research Group, Home Office.

BUZAWA, E.S. and BUZAWA, C.G. (1993) 'The Impact of Arrest on Domestic Violence'. *American Behavioural Scientist*, Vol. 36, No. 5, pp.558-574.

CAHN, N.R. and LERMAN, L.G. (1991) 'Prosecuting Woman Abuse' in STEINMAN, M. (ed) *Woman Battering: Policy Responses*. Cincinnati: Anderson Publishing Co.

COMPTON, P. (1995) *Demographic Review Northern Ireland*. Belfast: NI Economic Council.

CRAIG, Y. (1992) 'Domestic Violence and Magistrates Courts', *Justice of the Peace*, Vol. 156, Pt 36, pp.568-570.

CRIME STATISTICS (1993) *Criminal Statistics, England and Wales*. London: HMSO.

CULF, A. (1995) 'Channel Four Reveals Courts Lenient to Wife Killers', *Guardian*, 13 September.

DAVIDOFF, L. and DOWDS, L. (1989) 'Recent trends in crimes of violence against the person in England and Wales', *Home Office Research and Planning Unit Research Bulletin*, No. 27.

DOBASH, R.P and DOBASH, R.E. (1979) *Violence Against Wives*. Shepton Mallet: Open Books.

DOBASH, R.E. and DOBASH, R.P. (1992) *Women, Violence and Social Change*. London: Routledge.

EDWARDS, S. (1986) 'The Real Risks of Violence behind Closed Doors', *New Law Journal*, 136/628:1191-1193.

EDWARDS, S. (1989) *Policing 'Domestic' Violence. Women, the Law and the State*, London: Sage Publications.

ELLIOT, D.S. (1989) Criminal Justice Procedures in Family Violence Crimes in L. Oklin & M. Elliott, D.S. (eds) *Family Violence*. Chicago: University of Chicago Press.

EVASON, E. (1982) *Hidden Violence*. Belfast: Farset Press.

FERRARO, K.J. (1989) 'Policing Women Battering', *Social Problems* Vol. 36, pp.61-74.

FERRARO, K.J. and BOYCHUK, T. (1992) 'The Court's response to interpersonal violence: A comparison of intimate and non-intimate assault', in E. Buzawa and C. Buzawa (eds) *Domestic Violence: The changing criminal justice response*. Westport: Greenwood.

FERRARO, K.J. (1995) 'Domestic Violence and the Criminal Justice Response', *American Society of Criminology Task Force on Domestic Violence for US Attorney General*.

FINEMAN, M.A. and MUKITIUK, R. (1994) *Public Nature of Private Violence*. New York: Routledge.

FORD, D.A. (1995) 'Domestic Violence against Women', unpublished paper, Indiana University.

FORD, D.A. and REGOLI, M.J. (1993) 'The Criminal Prosecution of Wife Assaulters: Process, Problems and Effects', in N.Z. HILTON, (ed) *Legal Responses to Wife Assault*. New York, Sage Publications.

GELLES, R.J. (1993) 'Constraints against Family Violence: How Well Do They Work?' *American Behavioural Scientist*, Vol.5, pp.575-586.

GELLES, R.J. and CONTE, J.R. (1990) 'Domestic Violence and Sexual Abuse of Children: a review of research in the eighties', *Journal of Marriage and Family*, Vol. 52, pp.1045-1058.

GRACE, S. (1995) *Policing Domestic Violence in the 1990s*. London: HMSO Home Office Research and Planning Unit Report 139.

HAGUE, G. and MALOS, E. (1993) *Domestic Violence: Action for Change*. Gloucester: New Clarion Press.

HART, B. (1993) 'Battered Women and the Criminal Justice System', *American Behavioural Scientist*, Vol. 36, No 5, pp.624-638.

HORDER, J. (1992) *Provocation and Responsibility*. Oxford: Clarendon Press.

HORDER, J. (1995) 'Defences for Battered Women who Kill', unpublished paper, Worcester College, Oxford.

KANE, P (1995) *Policing and Wife Assault*, Unpublished MSc thesis. Jordanstown: University of Ulster.

KELLY, L (1994) *Victim Witness Support*, Unpublished Report on Study Visit to London, Ontario. North London University, Child Abuse Studies Unit.

KEWLEY, A. and CROMACK, V. (1994) *The Interagency Response to Domestic Violence in Hull: Final Report*. Hull: Home Office/Hull Safer Cities Project.

LERMAN, L.G. (1992) 'The Decontextualization of Domestic Violence', *Journal of Criminal Law and Criminology*, Vol. 83, No. 1, pp.217-240.

LOGUE, R. (1989) 'Legal Remedies for Domestic Violence', unpublished paper. Coleraine: Centre For Research On Women, University of Ulster.

McWILLIAMS, M. and McKIERNAN, J. (1993) *Bringing It Out In The Open: Domestic Violence in Northern Ireland*. Belfast: HMSO.

MAHONEY, M.R. (1994) 'Victimization or Oppression? Women's lives, violence and agency', in Fineman, M.A. & Mykitiuk (ed) *The Public Nature of Private Violence*. New York: Routledge.

MERCER, E. (1993) *A Review of the Strategy and Effectiveness of the new RUC policy on domestic violence*. Unpublished MSc thesis. Jordanstown: University of Ulster.

MONTGOMERY, P. and BELL, V. (1986) *Police Response to Wife Assault: A Northern Ireland Study*, Belfast: NI Women's Aid Federation.

MOONEY, J. (1994) *The Hidden Figure: Domestic Violence in North London*. London: Islington Council/Middlesex University.

MORLEY, R. and MULLENDER, A. (1992) 'Hype or Hope? The Importation of Pro-Arrest Policies and Batterers' Programmes from North America to Britain as Key Measures for Preventing Violence against Women in the Home', *International Journal of Law and the Family*, No. 6, pp.265-88.

MORLEY, R. and MULLENDER, A. (1994) *Preventing Domestic Violence To Women*. London: Home Office Police Research Group, Paper No.48.

MURPHY, P (1995) 'Evidence of Extraneous Acts and Disposition' in P Murphy *Evidence*. London: Blackstone Press.

PENCE, E. (1989) *The Justice System's Response to Domestic Assault Cases: a guide for policy development*. Duluth: DAIP Minnesota Program Development Inc.

POLSBY, D.D. (1992) 'Suppressing Domestic Violence with Law Reforms', *Journal of Criminal Law and Criminology*, Vol. 83, No. 1, pp.250-53.

QUINN, D. (1991) 'The Legal Response to Domestic Violence in Northern Ireland' in *Domestic Violence and the Law Conference Report*. Belfast: N.I.Women's Aid Federation.

RADFORD, J & Kelly, L (1995) 'Self-Preservation and Feminist Jurisprudence, in N. Maynard & J. Purvis (ed) *Heterosexual Politics*. London: Taylor and Francis.

SANDERS, A. (1988) 'Personal Violence and Public Order: A Prosecution of 'Domestic' Violence in England and Wales', *International Journal of the Sociology of Law*, No 16, pp.359-382.

SCHMIDT, J.D. and SHERMAN, L.W. (1993) 'Does Arrest Deter Domestic Violence?', *American Behavioural Scientist*, Vol. 36, No. 5, pp.601-609.

SMITH, D.J. (1994) *Domestic Violence: a policing priority?* Unpublished MBA dissertation. Liverpool: John Moores University.

SMITH, L.J.P. (1989) *Domestic Violence*. London: HMSO Home Office Research Study 107.

STARK, E. (1993) 'Mandatory Arrest of Batterers: a reply to its critics'. *American Behavioural Scientist*, Vol. 36, No. 5, pp.651-680.

VICTIM SUPPORT (1992) *Domestic Violence: Report of a National Inter-Agency Working Party*. London: Victim Support.

WALKER, J and McNICOL, L. (1994) *Policing Domestic Violence: Protection, Prevention or Prudence?* Newcastle: Relate Centre for Family Studies.

WALLACE, A. (1986) *Homicide: The Social Reality*. Sydney: New South Wales Bureau of Crime Statistics and Research.

WEST YORKSHIRE POLICE (1995) *Surveys of Domestic Violence: 1990-1993*. Wakefield: West Yorkshire Police.

WEST YORKSHIRE POLICE (1995) 'Homicide Data 1990-1995', unpublished paper. Wakefield: West Yorkshire Police.

WILSON, M. and DALY, M. (1992) 'Who kills whom in spousal homicide? On the exceptional sex ratio of spousal homicides in the United States', *Criminology*, 30:301-327.

WILSON, M. and DALY, M. (1994) 'Spousal Homicide', *Statistics Canada*, Vol.14 No.8.

WILSON, M., DALY, M. and WRIGHT, C. (1993) 'Uxoricide in Canada: Demographic risk patterns', Canadian Journal of Criminology, Vol.35, pp.263-291.